PIANO • VOCAL • GUITAR

Bob Seger
& THE SILVER BULLET BAND
GREATEST HITS 2

T0052896

Front cover photo by Caroline Greyshock
Back cover photo by Terrance Bert

ISBN 0-634-06887-3

HAL•LEONARD®
CORPORATION
7777 W. BLUEMOUND RD. P.O. BOX 13819 MILWAUKEE, WI 53213

Visit Hal Leonard Online at
www.halleonard.com

UNDERSTANDING

Words and Music by
BOB SEGER

Medium tempo

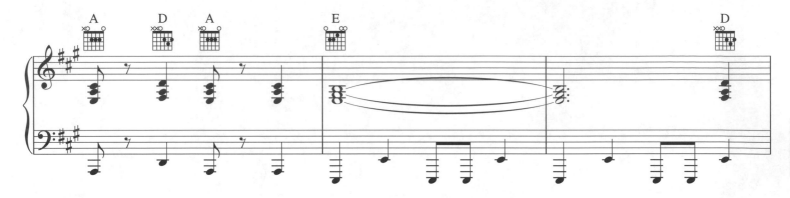

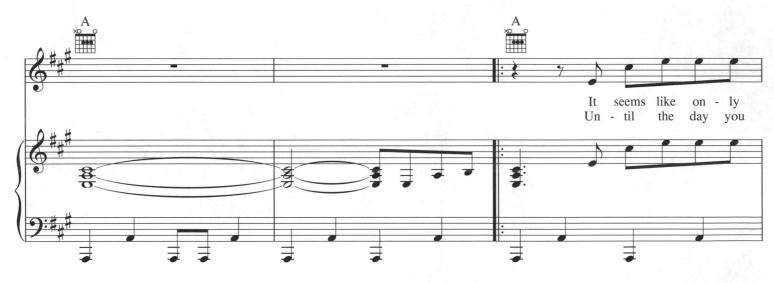

It seems like on - ly
Un - til the day you

yes - ter - day   I did - n't have a clue. ___
came a - long,   I used to just get lost. ___

stand - ing.   You've giv - en me some pride. ___

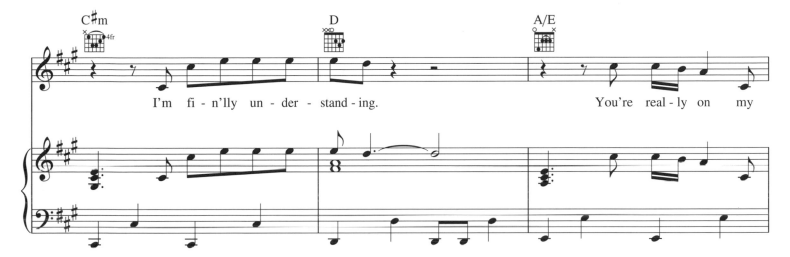

I'm fi - n'lly un - der - stand - ing.   You're real - ly on my

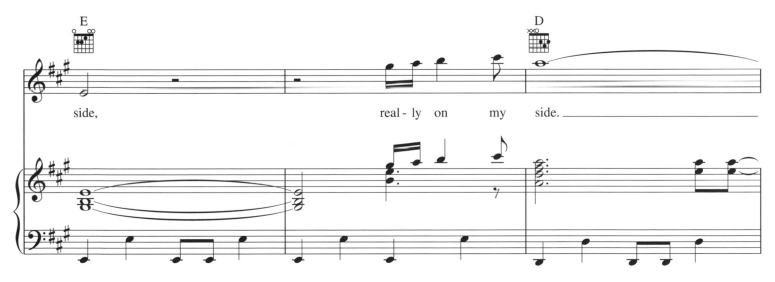

side,   real - ly on my side. ___

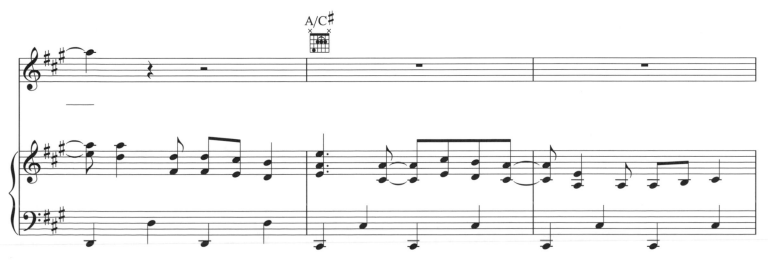

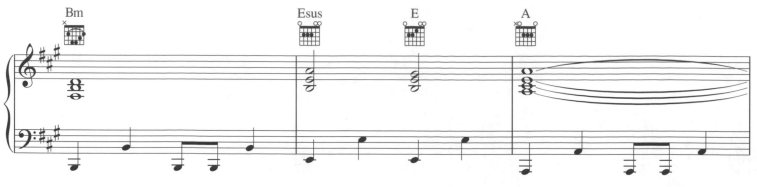

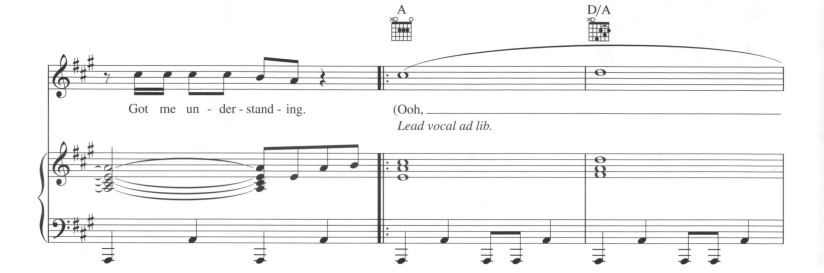

Got me un - der - stand - ing.　　　(Ooh, _____

Lead vocal ad lib.

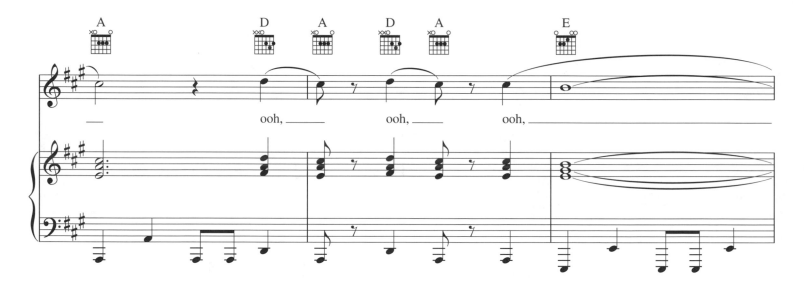

ooh, _____　ooh, _____　ooh, _____

Repeat and Fade

_____　you got me un - der - stand - ing.)

THE FIRE DOWN BELOW

Words and Music by
BOB SEGER

All through the shad - ows,   aw,   they come and they go ___
When it all gets too heav - y   that's when they come and they go ___

with on - ly one thing in com - mon:

they got the fire down be - low. ___

Solo ends

Well, it hap - pens out in Ve - gas,   hap - pens in Mo - line,   on the

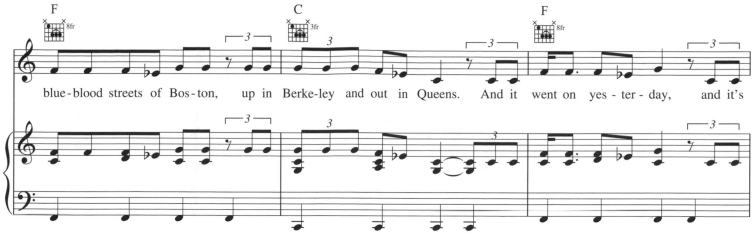

blue-blood streets of Bos - ton, up in Berke-ley and out in Queens. And it went on yes - ter - day, and it's

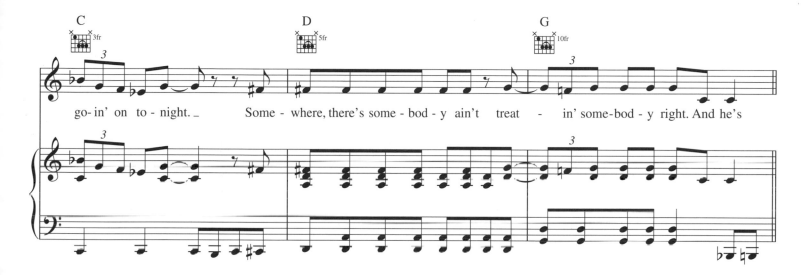

go - in' on to - night. _ Some - where, there's some - bod - y ain't treat - in' some-bod - y right. And he's

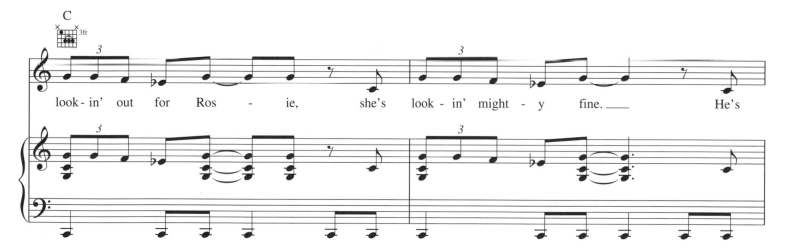

look - in' out for Ros - ie, she's look - in' might - y fine. _____ He's

walk - in' the streets for Nan - cy. He'll find her ev - 'ry time. And when the street lights _ flick - er,

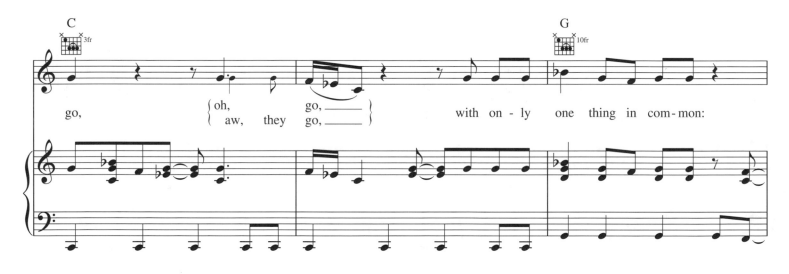

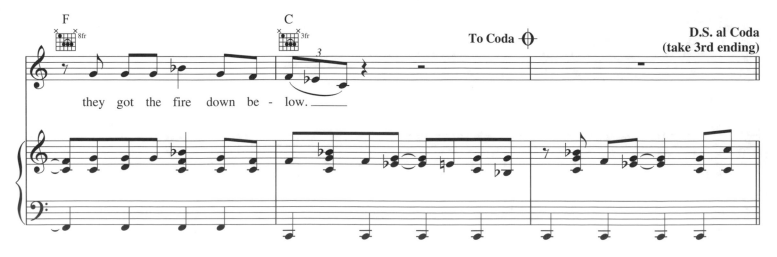

HER STRUT

Words and Music by
BOB SEGER

Moderate Rock

N.C.

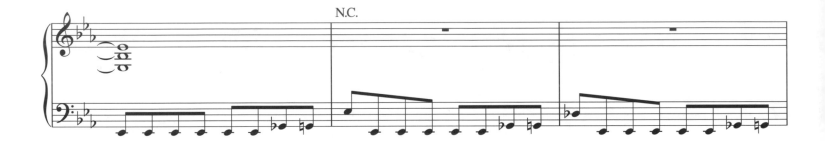

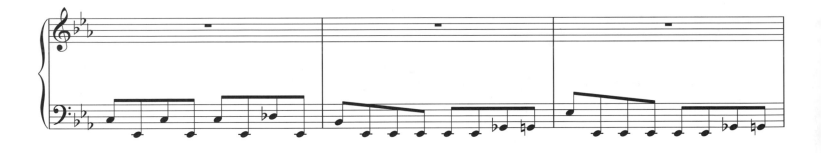

She's

E♭5

to - tal - ly ___ com - mit - ted   to ma - jor in - de - pen - dence.
times they'll want ___ to leave her,   just give up ___ and leave her,   but

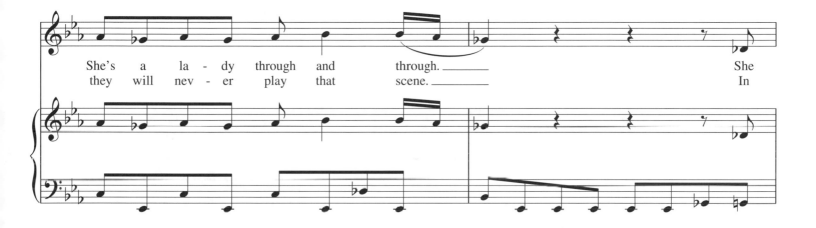

She's a la - dy through and through. _____   She
they will nev - er play that scene. _____   In

gives them quite a bat - tle,   all ____ that they can han - dle. She'll
spite of all their talk - ing,   once she starts in walk - ing, the

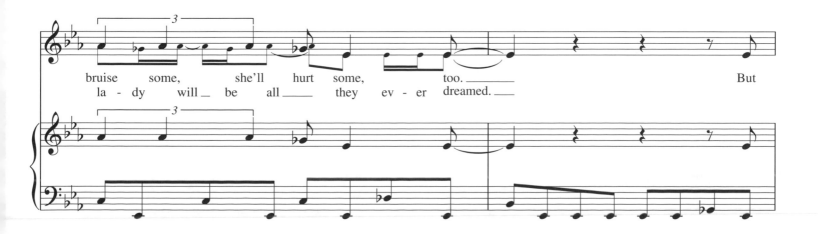

bruise some, she'll hurt some, too. _____   But
la - dy will ___ be all ___ they ev - er dreamed. ___

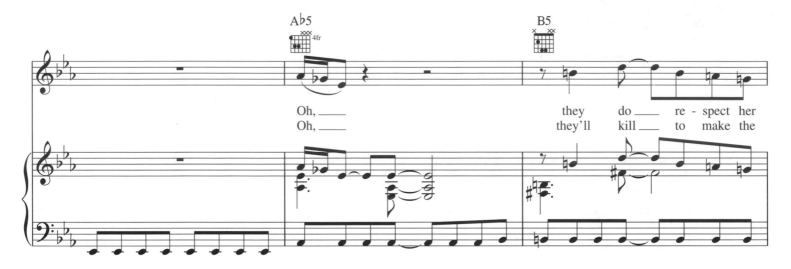

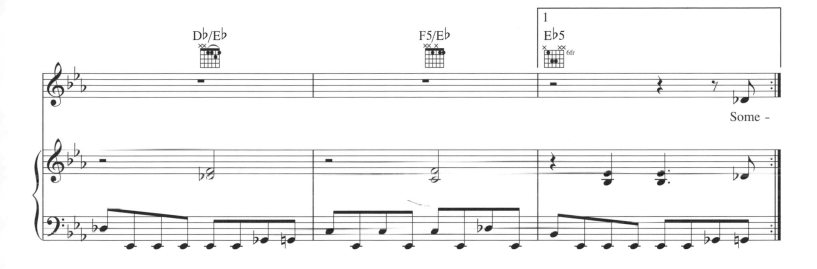

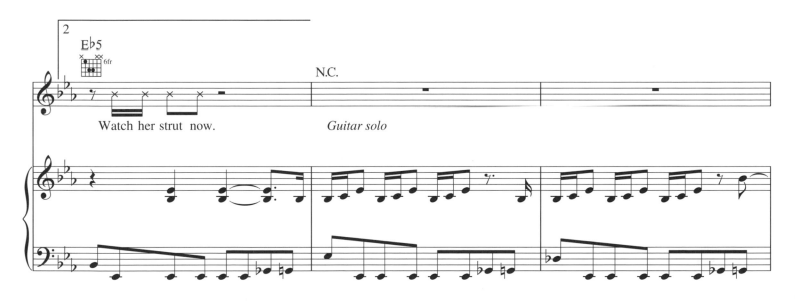

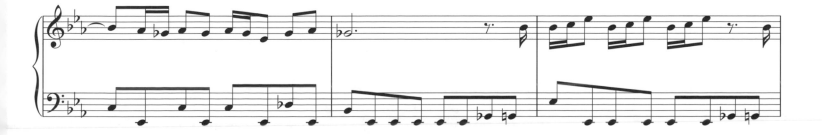

Oh, _____ they love ___ to watch her strut. _____

Solo ends

Oh, _____ they do ___ re - spect her,

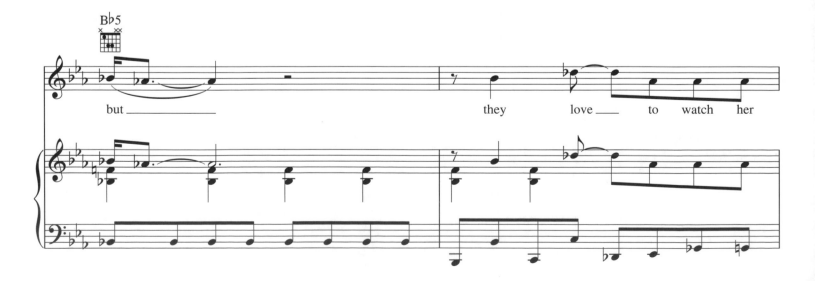

but _____ they love ___ to watch her

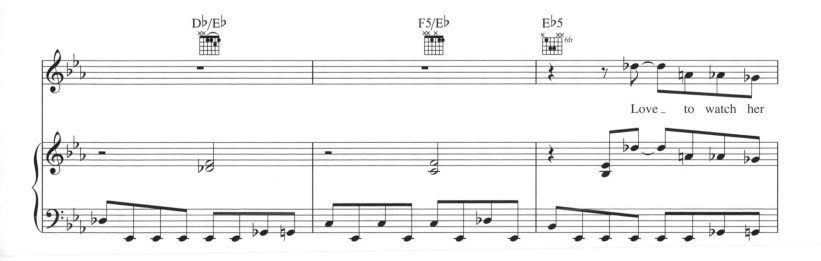

BEAUTIFUL LOSER

Words and Music by
BOB SEGER

Beau - ti - ful ___ los - er, ___ where ___ you gon - na
Beau - ti - ful ___ los - er, ___ read ___ it on the
End instrumental Beau - ti - ful ___ los - er, ___ nev - er take it

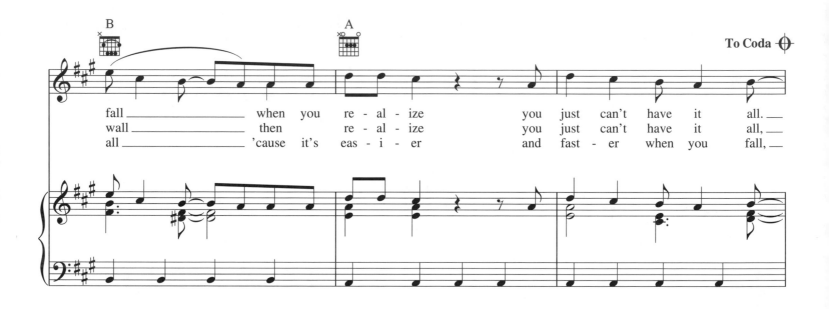

fall _____ when you re - al - ize you just can't have it all. ___
wall _____ then re - al - ize you just can't have it all, ___
all _____ 'cause it's eas - i - er and fast - er when you fall, ___

To Coda ⊕

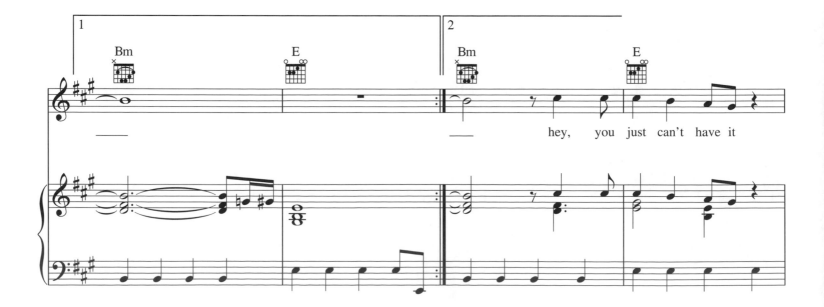

1
___

2
___ hey, you just can't have it

all. _____ You can't have it all. ____

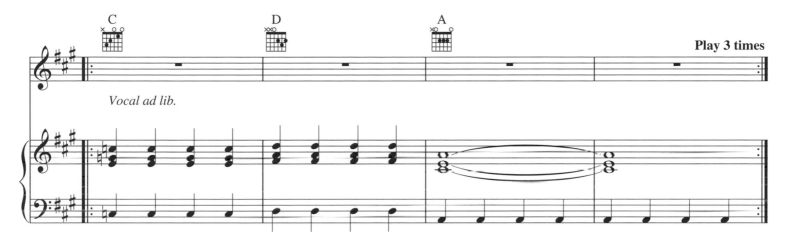

Play 3 times

Vocal ad lib.

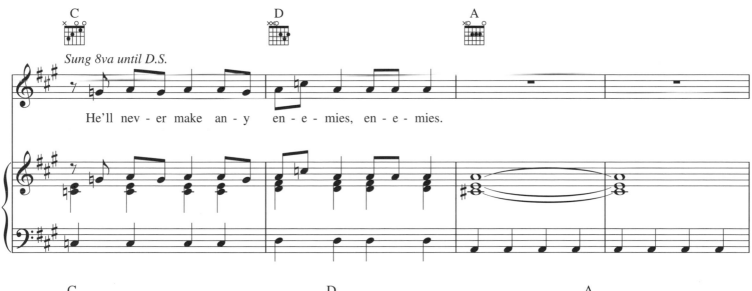

Sung 8va until D.S.

He'll nev- er make an- y en- e- mies, en- e- mies.

He won't com- plain if he's caught in a freeze. _____

22

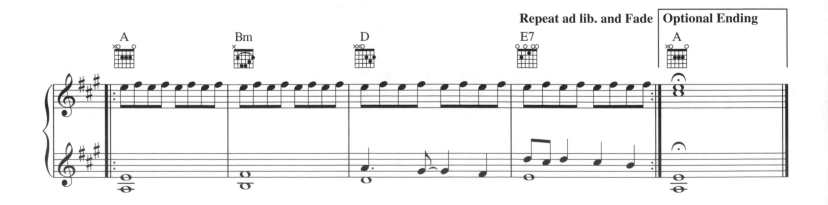

SUNSPOT BABY

Words and Music by
BOB SEGER

She gave me a false ad - dress, ___ took off ___

___ with my A - mer - i - can Ex - press. ___ Sun - spot ba - by, she

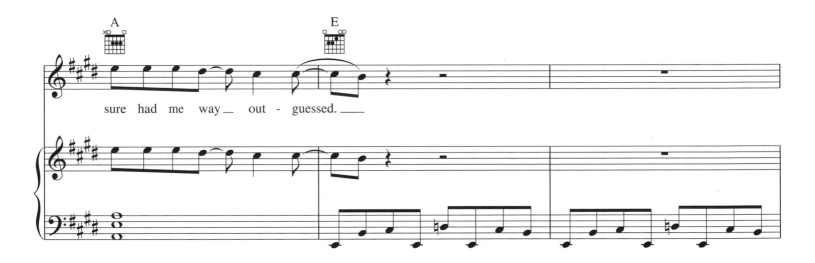

sure had me way ___ out - guessed. ___

She left me here strand - ed like a

dog out in the yard. _____

Charged up a for - tune on my cred - it card. _____

She used my ad - dress ___ and my name. ___

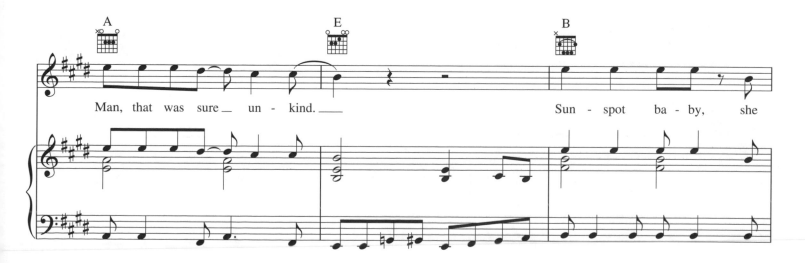

Man, that was sure ___ un - kind. ___ Sun - spot ba - by, she

sure had a real___ good time.___ I

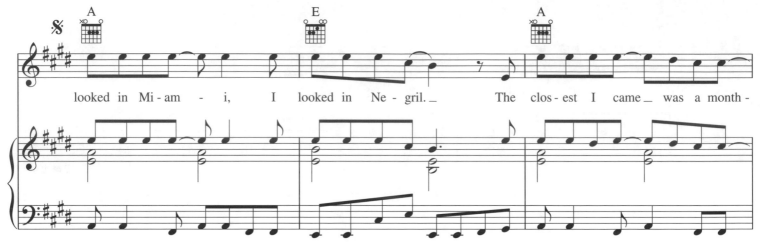

looked in Mi-am-i, I looked in Ne-gril.___ The clos-est I came___ was a month-

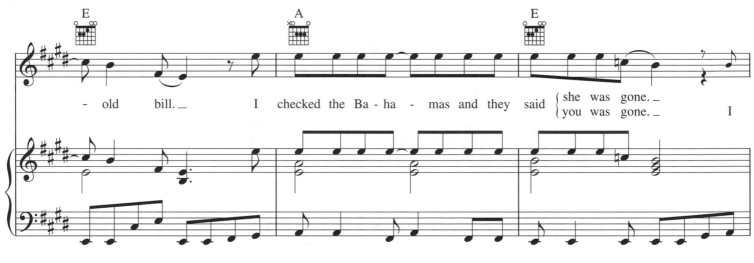

-old bill.___ I checked the Ba-ha-mas and they said { she was gone.___ / you was gone.___ } I

Can't un-der-stand___ why she did___ me so wrong. But she packed up her bags,___ she
can't un-der-stand___ why she did___ me so wrong. But she packed up her bags,___ and she

took off down the road. _____ She
took off down the road. _____ She

said she was go - ing to vis - it sis - ter Flo. _____
left me here strand - ed with the bills she owed. _____

'Cause she used my ad - dress ___ and my name ___ and,
She used my ad - dress ___ and my name. ___

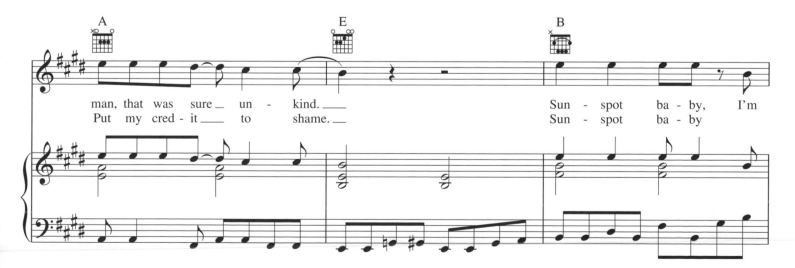

man, that was sure un - kind. ____ Sun - spot ba - by, I'm
Put my cred - it ___ to shame. ___ Sun - spot ba - by

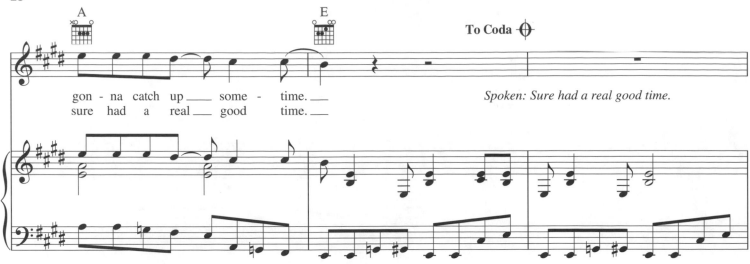

gon - na catch up ___ some - time. ___
sure had a real ___ good time. ___

Spoken: Sure had a real good time.

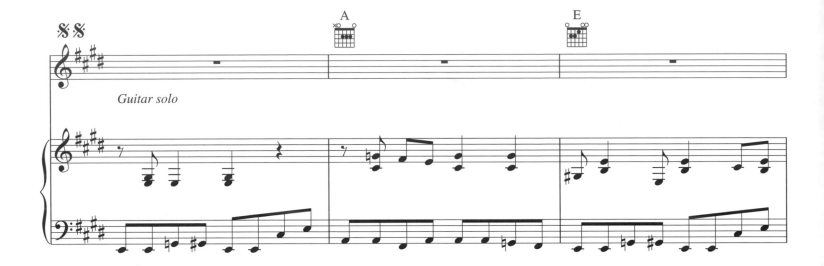

Guitar solo

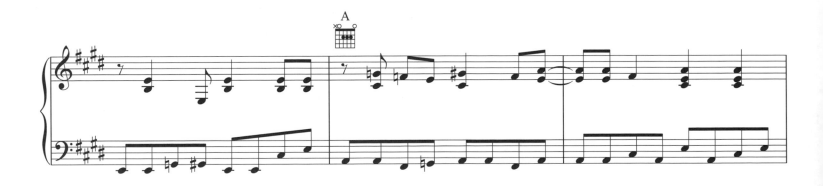

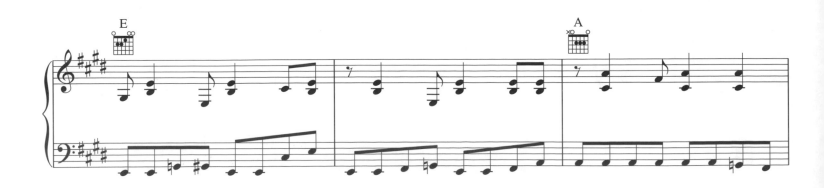

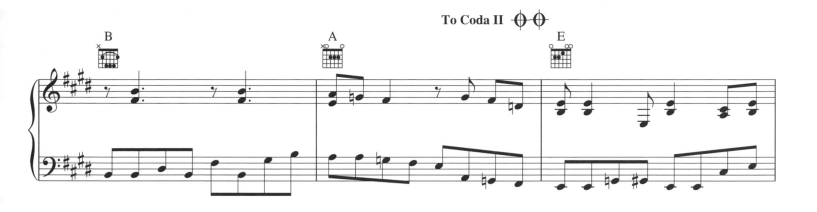

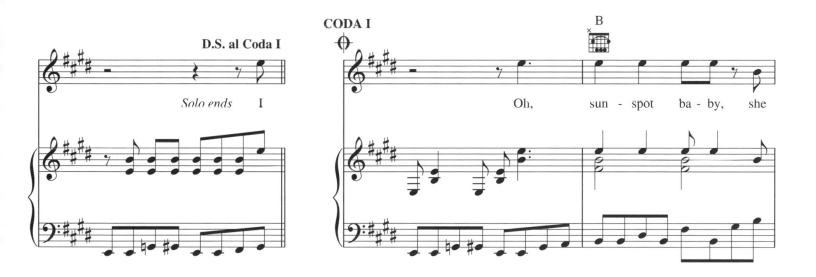

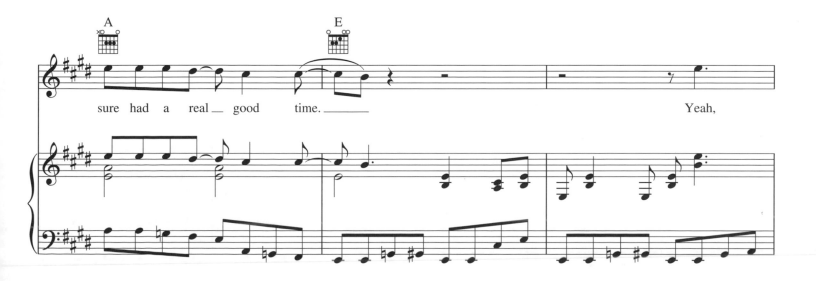

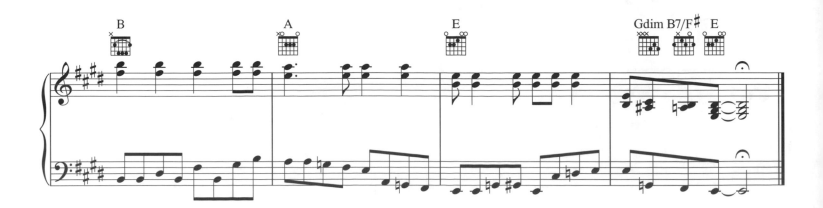

KATMANDU

Words and Music by
BOB SEGER

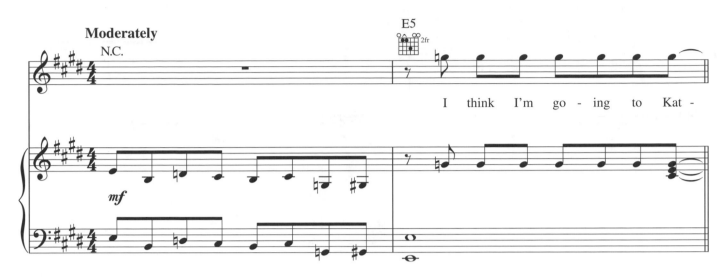

I think I'm go-ing to Kat -

- man - du, _____ that's real - ly, real - ly where I'm
(2., 3.) - man - du, _____ up to the moun - tains where I'm

go - ing to. _____ If I ev - er get out _____ of here, _____
go - ing to. _____ Hey, if I ev - er get out _____ of here, _____

that's what I'm gon-na do.____   K K K K K K Kat-

-man - du,____
{ I think that's real-ly where I'm go - ing to.____ }
{ real-ly, real-ly where I'm go - ing to.____ }
{ take me, ba-by, 'cause I'm go - ing with_ you._ }

(1.-3.) If I ev-er get out____ of here,____   I'm goin' to Kat-man - du._

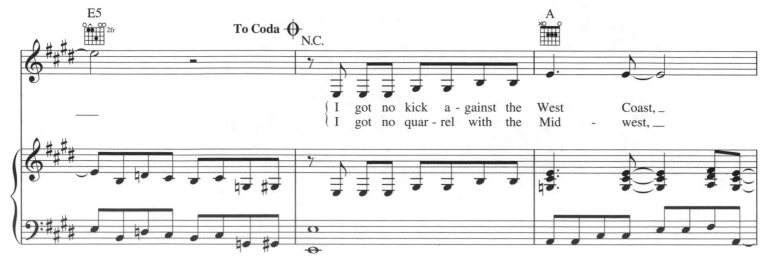

To Coda   N.C.

{ I got no kick a - gainst the West   Coast, _ }
{ I got no quar - rel with the Mid - west, _ }

and to my-self be true.____
I'm tired of be - ing blue.____

That's why I'm go - ing to Kat -

D.S. al Coda

That's why I'm go - ing to Kat -

CODA

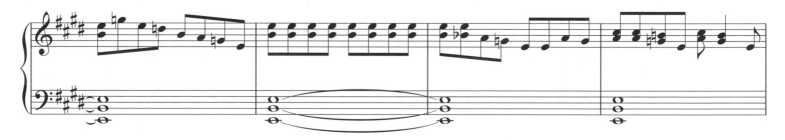

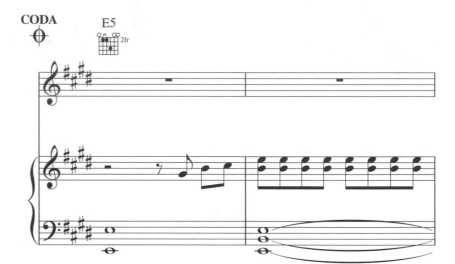

Instrumental solo

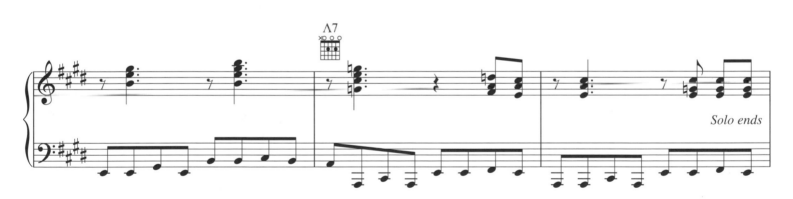

Solo ends

I ain't got noth - in' 'gainst the East Coast. _

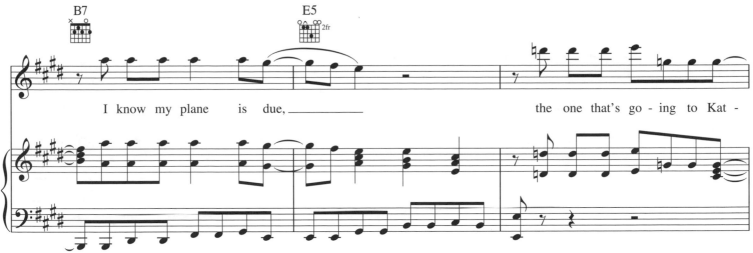

I know my plane is due, _____ the one that's go - ing to Kat -

- man - du, __ up to the moun - tains where I'm go - ing to. _____

If I ev - er get out ___ of here, _____ that's what I'm gon - na do. ___

___ K K K K K K Kat - man - du, __

real - ly, real - ly, real - ly go - ing to._____ If I ev - er get out

____ of here,_____ if I ev - er get out____ of here,_____

if I ev - er get out____ of here,_____ I'm going to Kat - man - du.__

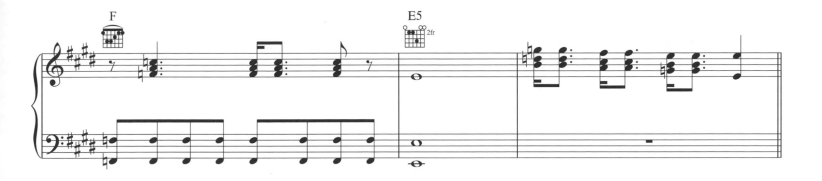

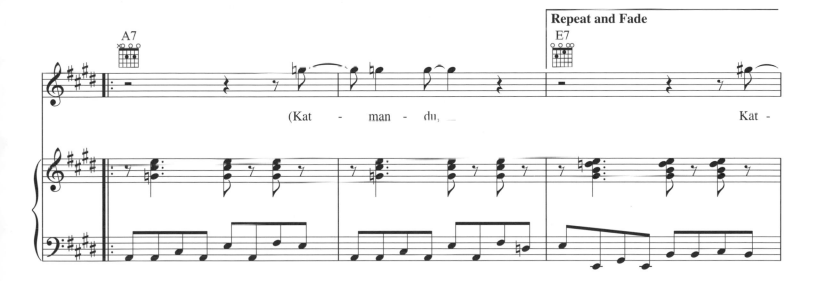

Repeat and Fade

(Kat - man - du, Kat -

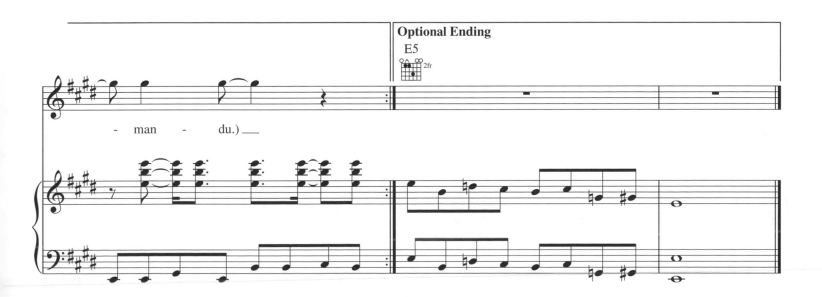

Optional Ending

- man - du.)

SHAME ON THE MOON

Words and Music by
RODNEY CROWELL

Moderately

Un - til you've been ___ be - side a
Once in - side ___ a wom - an's
Ev - 'ry - where ___ it's all a -

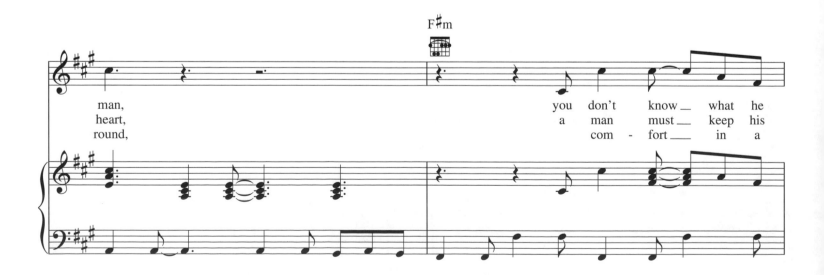

man,   you don't know ___ what he
heart,   a man must ___ keep his
round,   com - fort ___ in a

wants.   You don't   know   if he
head.   Heav - en   o - pens
crowd.   Stran - gers'   fac - es

cries at night. _____   You don't   know   if he
up the door _____   where an - gels   fear to
all a - round, _____   laugh - in'   right out

don't.   When noth - in' ____ comes
tread.   Some men ____ go
loud.   Hey, watch where ___ you're

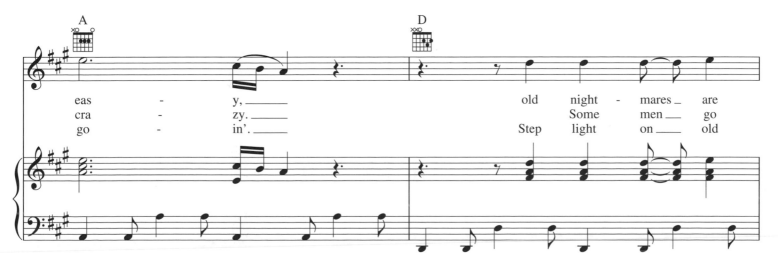

eas - y, ____   old night - mares ___ are
cra - zy. ____   Some men ___ go
go - in'. ____   Step light on ___ old

real.
slow.
toes,

Un - til you've been __ be - side a
Some men go __ just where they
'cause un - til you've been __ be - side a

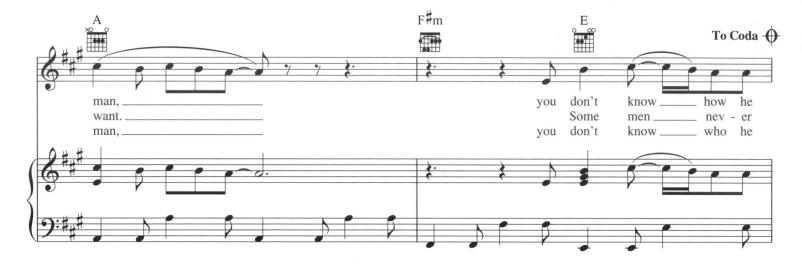

man, _____
want. _____
man, _____

you don't know ____ how he
Some men ____ nev - er
you don't know ____ who he

To Coda ⊕

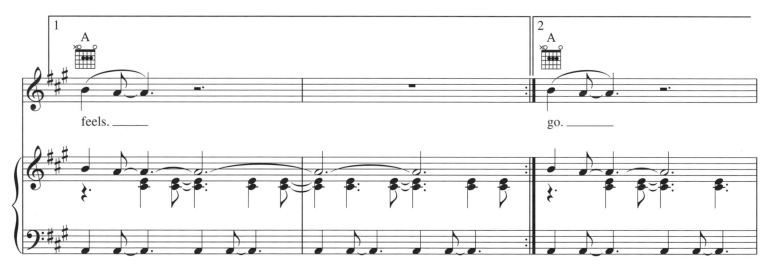

feels. ____

go. ____

Oh, _____

blame it on mid - night. ____

Ooh, _____ shame on _____ the

moon. _____

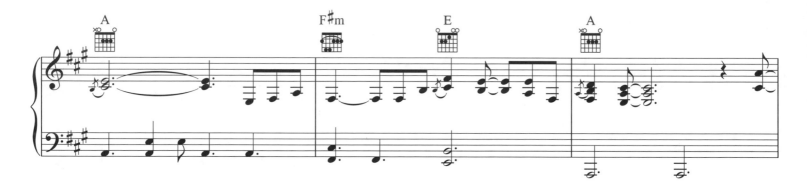

D.S. al Coda

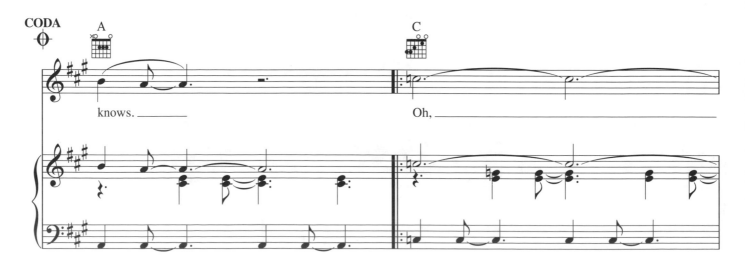

CODA

knows. _____

Oh, _____

blame it on mid - night. _____

Ooh, _____ shame on ____ the moon. ____

Repeat and Fade

Blame it on mid - night. _____
Shame on the moon. _____

Optional Ending

FIRE LAKE

Words and Music by
BOB SEGER

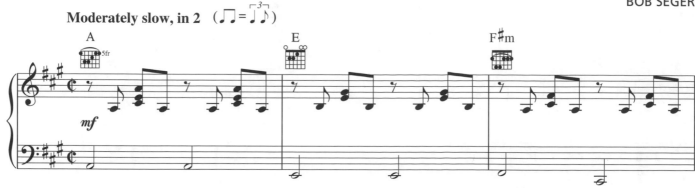

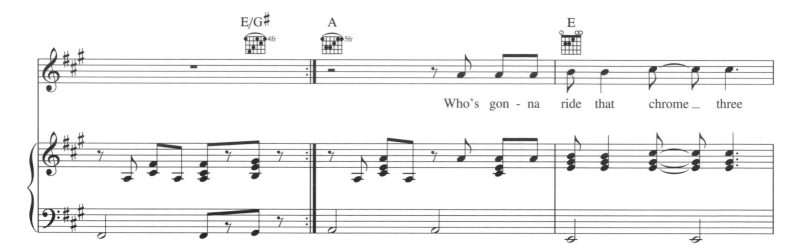

Who's gon - na ride that chrome __ three

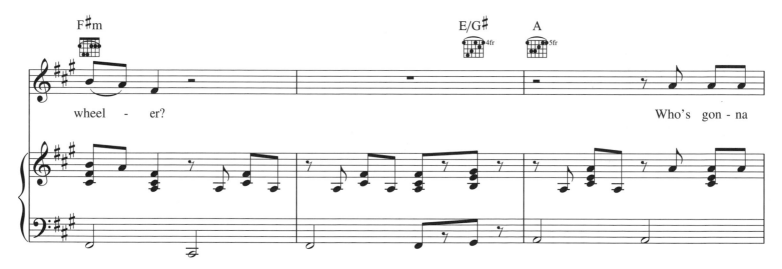

wheel - er?   Who's gon - na

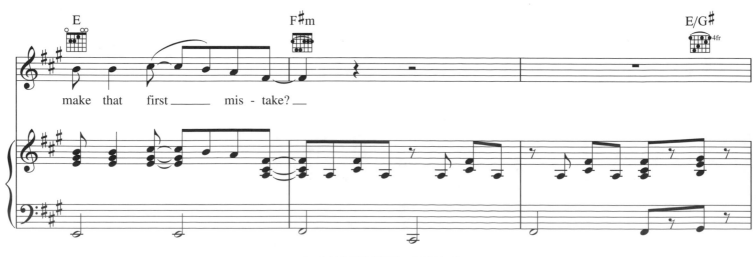

make that first _____ mis - take? __

Who wants to wear those gyp - sy leath -

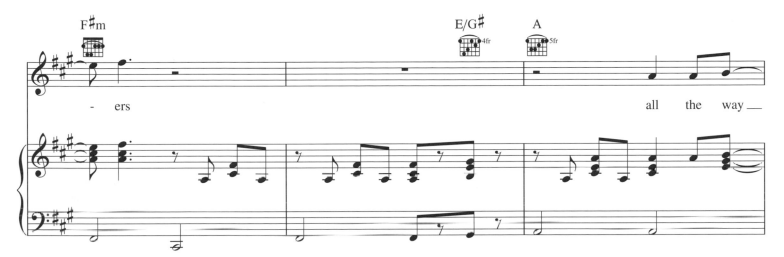

- ers   all the way ___

___ to Fire ___ Lake? _____

Who wants to break the news a - bout Un - cle Joe?

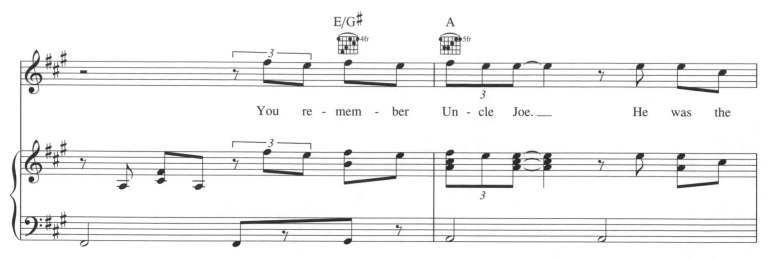

You re-mem-ber Un-cle Joe. ___ He was the

one a-fraid to cut the cake. ___

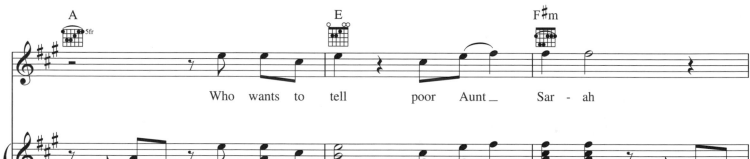

Who wants to tell poor Aunt ___ Sar-ah

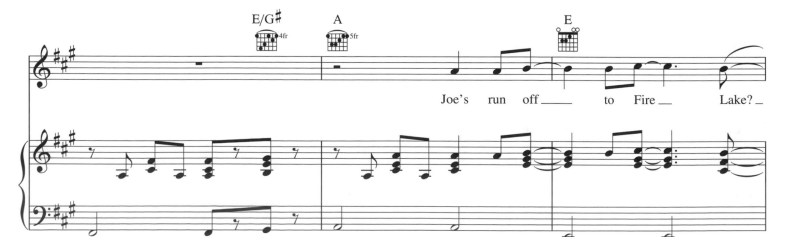

Joe's run off ____ to Fire ___ Lake? ___

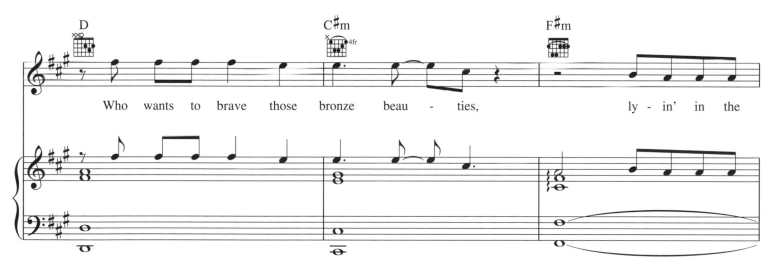

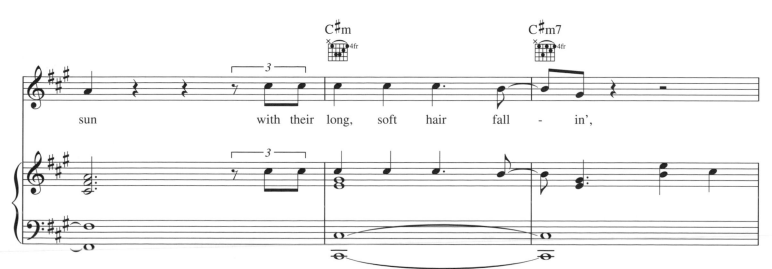

50

fly - in' as they run? Oh, they smile so shy and they

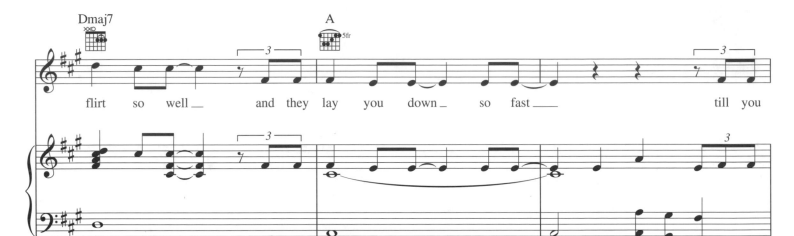

flirt so well ___ and they lay you down ___ so fast ___ till you

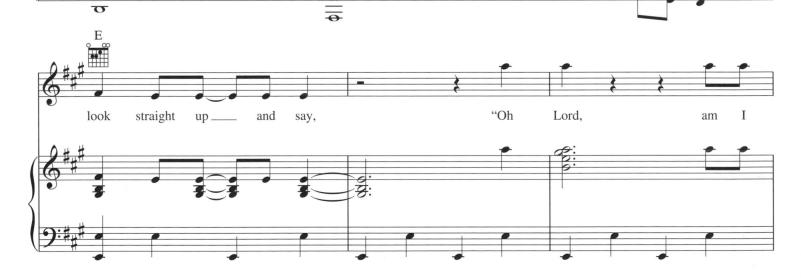

look straight up ___ and say, "Oh Lord, am I

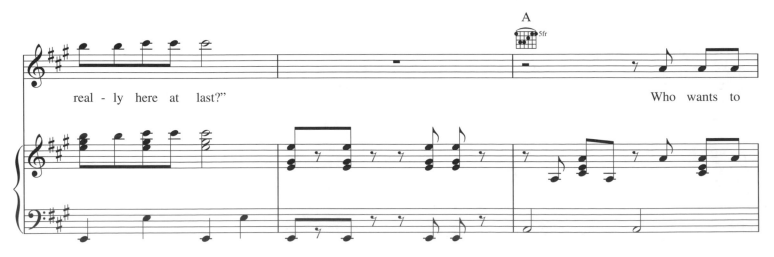

real - ly here at last?" Who wants to

play those eights __ and ac - es?

Who wants a raise? Who needs a stake? __

Who wants to take that long shot

gam - ble   and head out __

to Fire Lake?

(Who wants to go to Fire Lake?)

Lead vocal ad lib.

(Who wants to go to Fire Lake?)

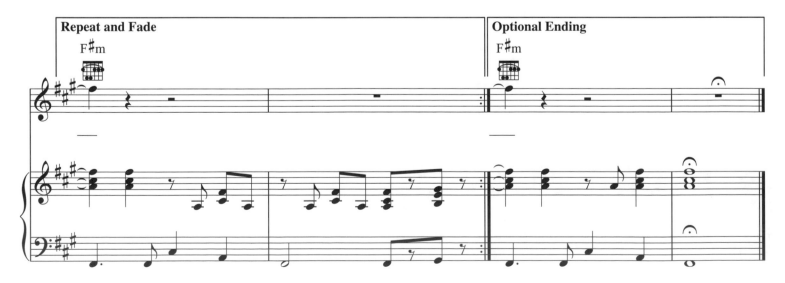

Repeat and Fade

Optional Ending

TRYIN' TO LIVE MY LIFE WITHOUT YOU

Words and Music by
EUGENE WILLIAMS

Moderate R&B

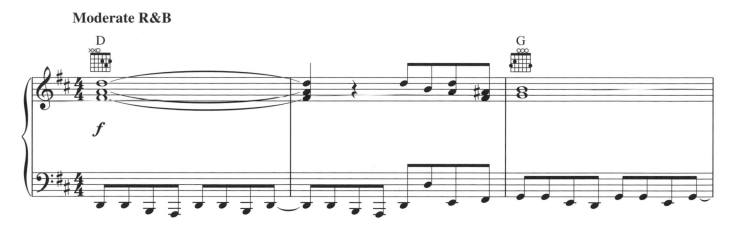

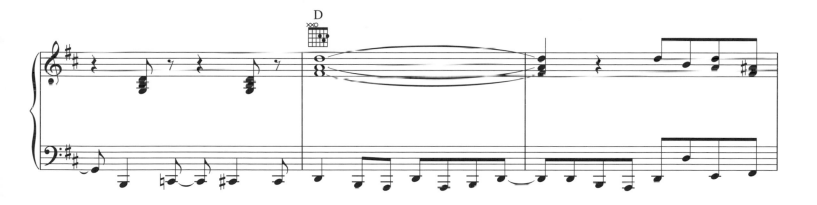

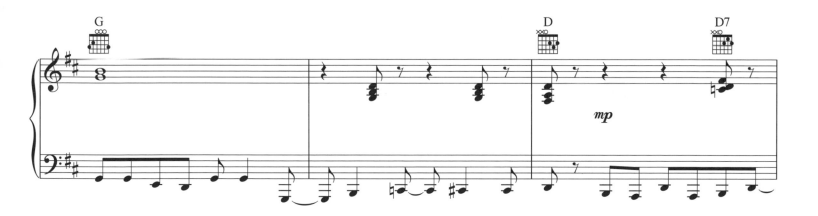

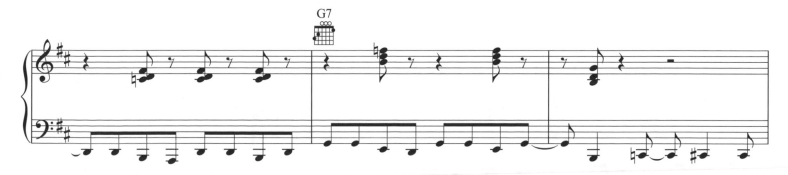

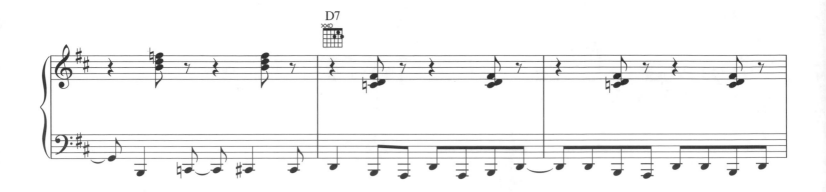

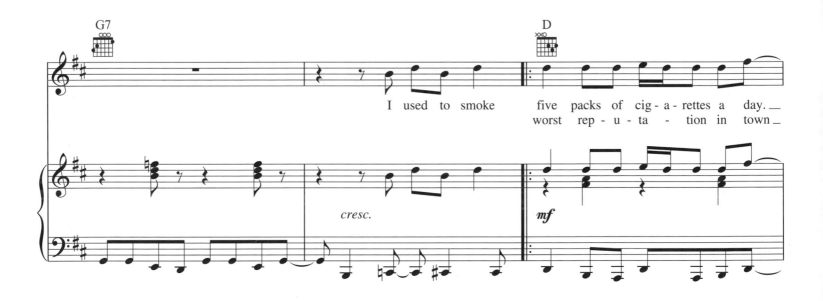

I used to smoke   five packs of cig-a-rettes a day. __
worst rep - u - ta - tion in town _

cresc.

mf

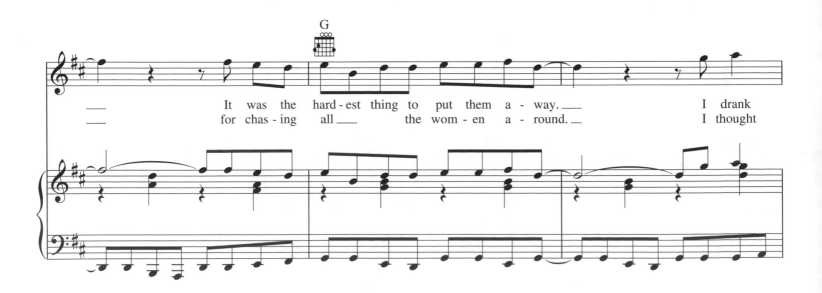

__ It was the hard-est thing to put them a - way. __   I drank
__ for chas - ing all __ the wom - en a - round. __   I thought

Tryin' to live my life with - out you, ___ babe. It's the hard -

- est thing I'll ev - er do.
(Hard - est thing I'll ev - er do.)

Tryin' to for - get the love we once shared, ___ yeah. ___ It's the hard -

- est bur - den I'll ev - er bear.
(Hard - est bur - den I'll ev - er bear.)

shared. ___ It's the hard - est bur - den I'll ev - er bear.
(Hard - est bur - den I'll

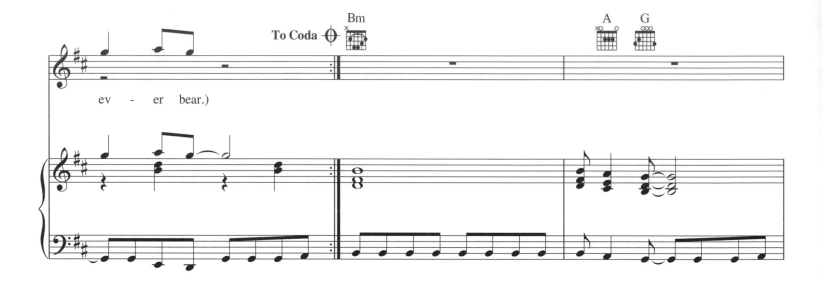

ev - er bear.)

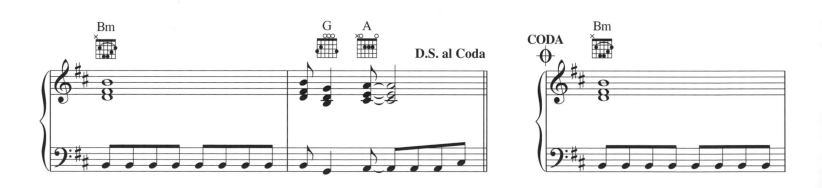

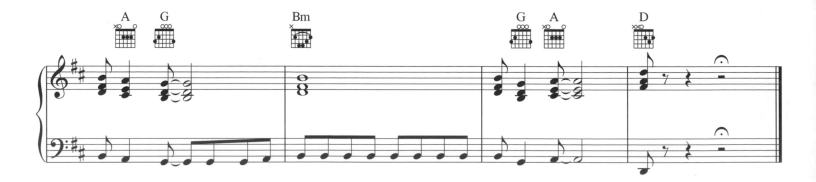

SHAKEDOWN
from the Paramount Motion Picture BEVERLY HILLS COP II

Words and Music by KEITH FORSEY,
HAROLD FALTERMEYER and BOB SEGER

Bright Rock

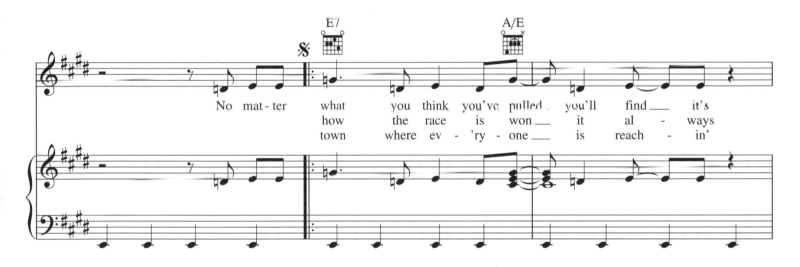

No mat-ter what you think you've pulled you'll find ___ it's
how the race is won ___ it al - ways
town where ev - 'ry - one ___ is reach - in'

not e - nough. ___ No mat-ter who you think you know, ___
ends the same. ___ An - oth - er room with - out a view ___
for the top. ___ This is a place where sec - ond best ___

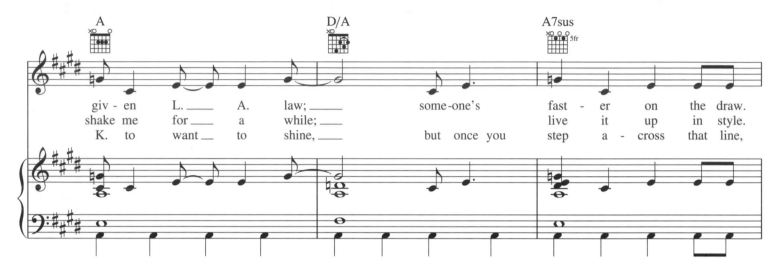

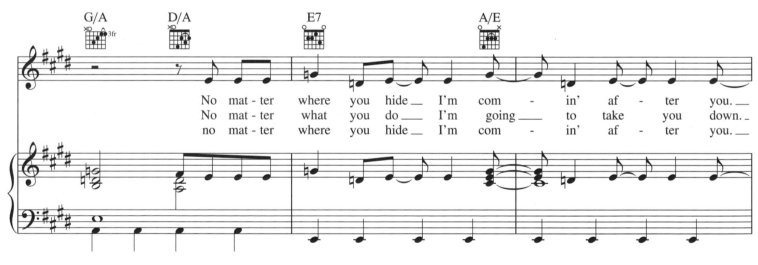

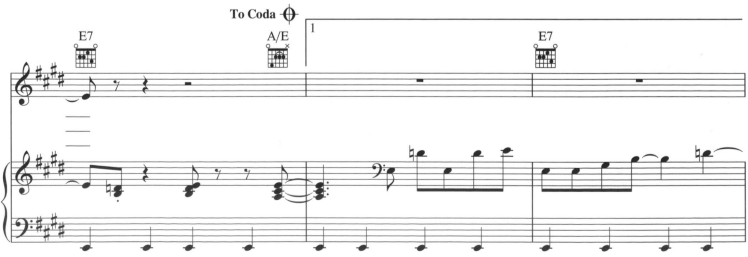

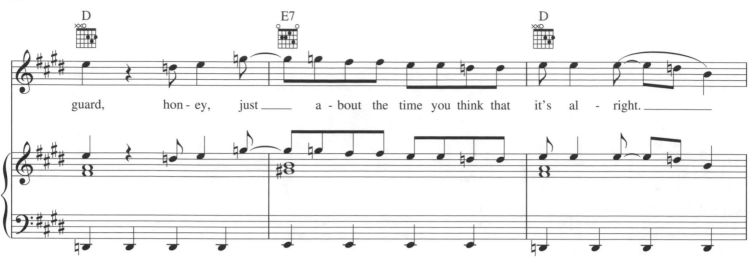

guard, hon - ey, just ____ a - bout the time you think that it's al - right. ____

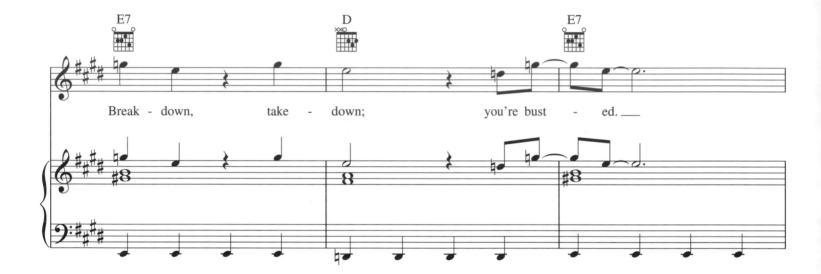

Break - down, take - down; you're bust - ed. ___

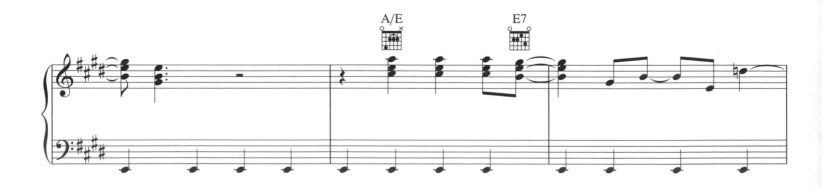

D.S. al Coda

This is a

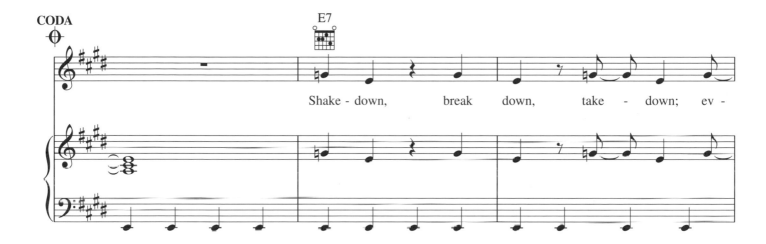

CODA

Shake - down, break down, take - down; ev -

- 'ry - bod - y wants in - to the crowd - ed light. _____ Break - down, take -

down; you're bust - ed. _____

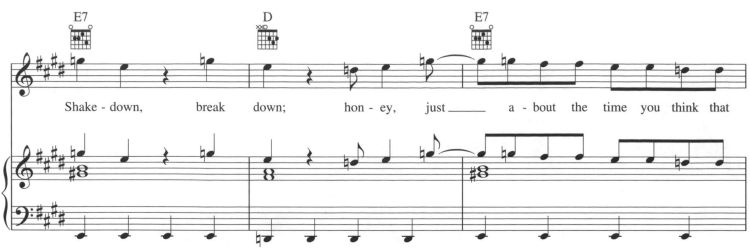

Shake - down, break down; hon - ey, just _____ a - bout the time you think that

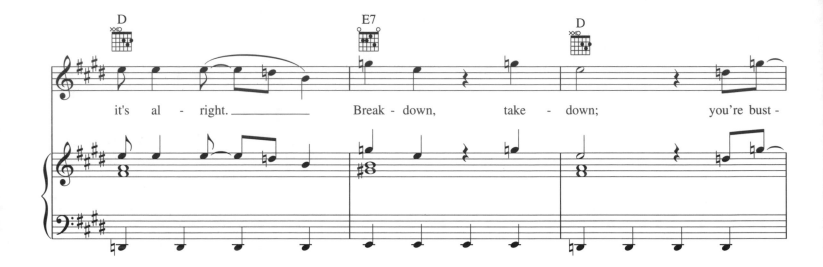

it's al - right. _____ Break - down, take - down; you're bust -

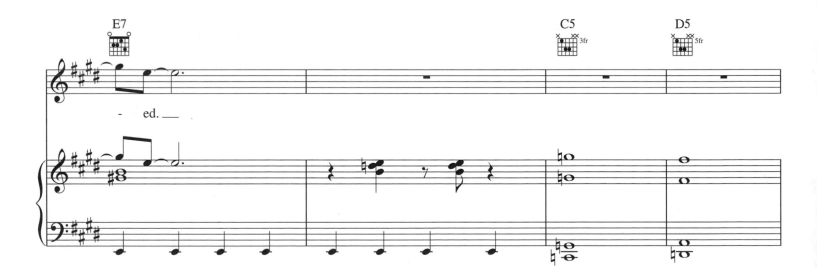

- ed. ___

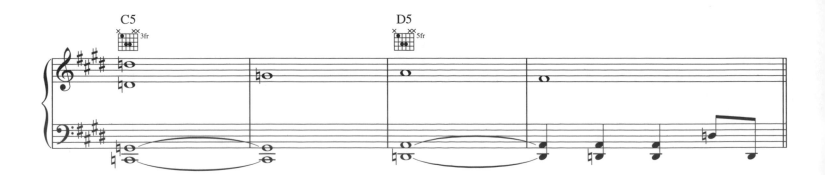

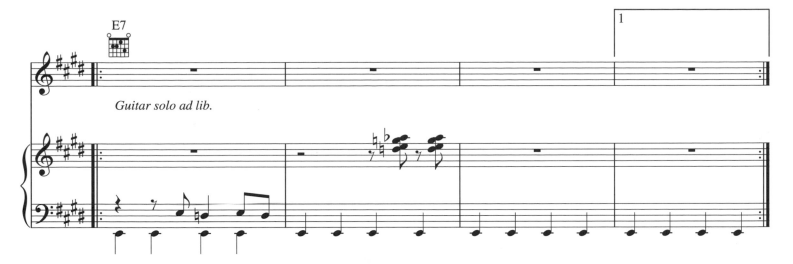

Guitar solo ad lib.

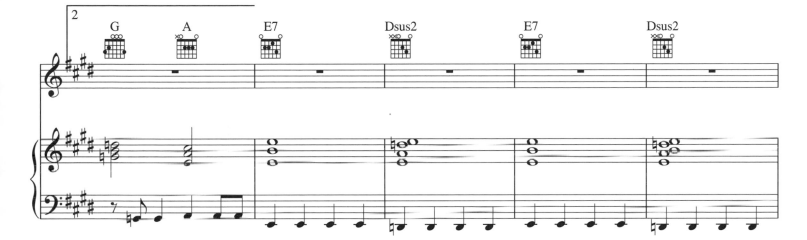

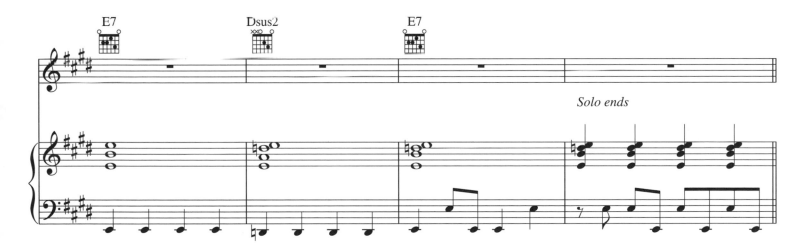

Solo ends

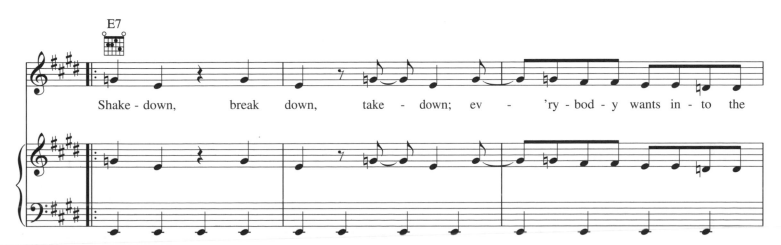

Shake - down, break down, take - down; ev - 'ry - bod - y wants in - to the

crowd - ed light. _____ Break - down, take - down; you're bust -

- ed. _____

(1., 3., . .) { Shake - down, break down; }
(2., 4., . .) { Let down break your guard, }

hon - ey, just _

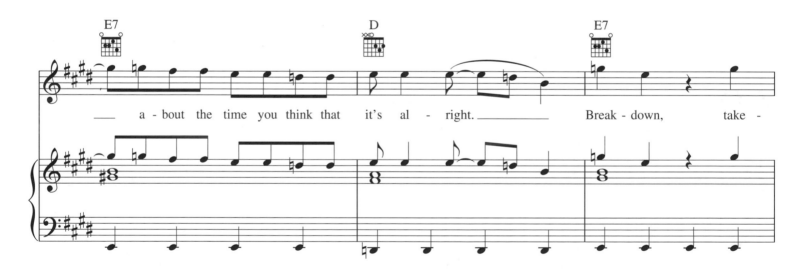

_____ a - bout the time you think that it's al - right. _____ Break - down, take -

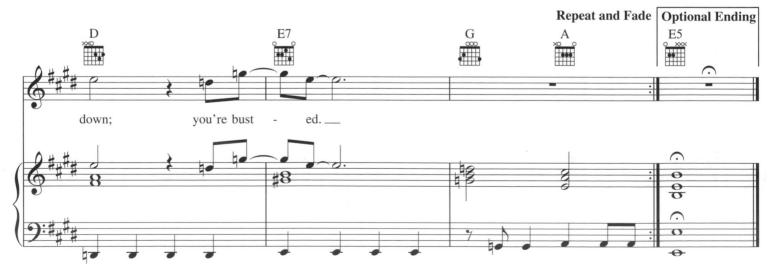

Repeat and Fade | **Optional Ending**

down; you're bust - ed. ___

MANHATTAN

Words and Music by
BOB SEGER

Moderate Rock

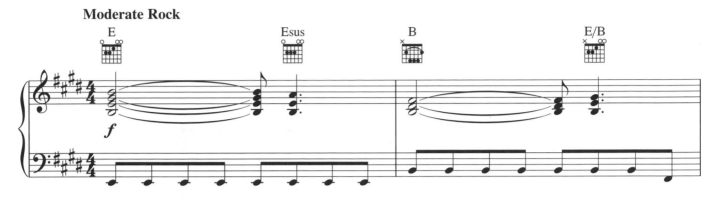

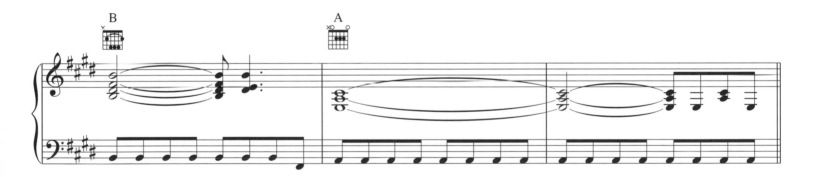

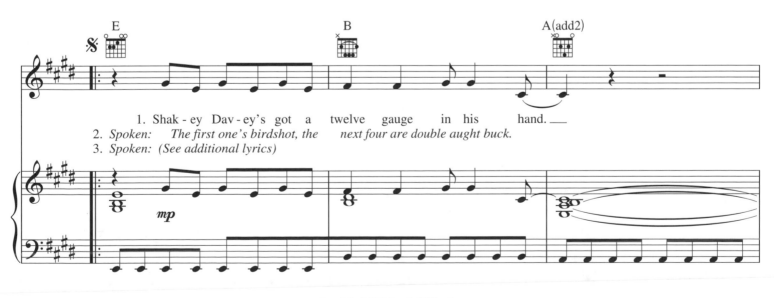

1. Shak - ey Dav - ey's got a twelve gauge in his hand. ___
2. *Spoken: The first one's birdshot, the next four are double aught buck.*
3. *Spoken: (See additional lyrics)*

It's sawed off to the lim - it.
The last one's a slug.

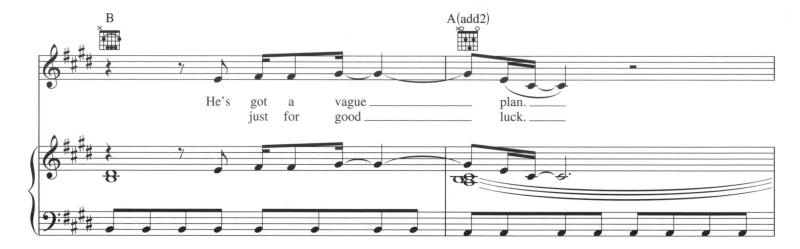

He's got a vague _____ plan. _____
just for good _____ luck. _____

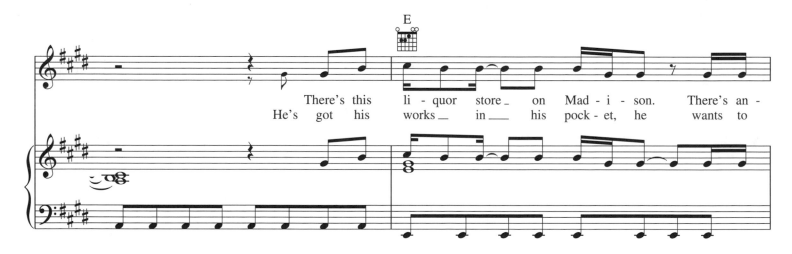

There's this li - quor store_ on Mad - i - son. There's an -
He's got his works_ in ___ his pock - et, he wants to

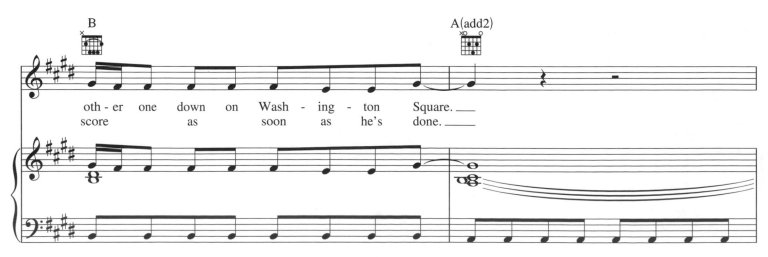

oth - er one down on Wash - ing - ton Square. __
score as soon as he's done. ____

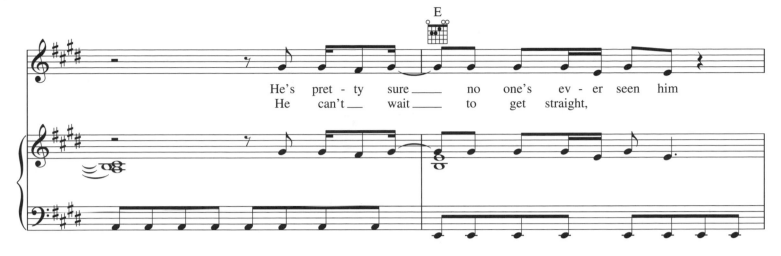

He's pret - ty sure ___ no one's ev - er seen him
He can't ___ wait ___ to get straight,

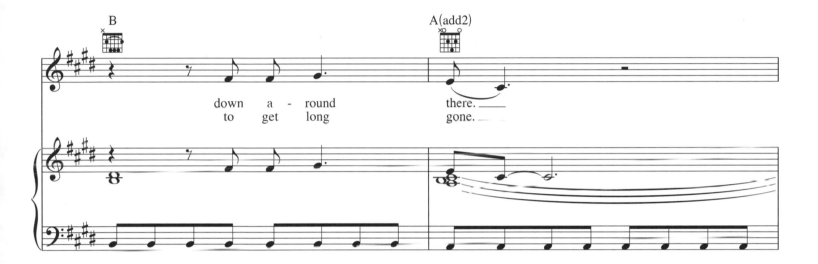

down a - round there. ___
to get long gone. ___

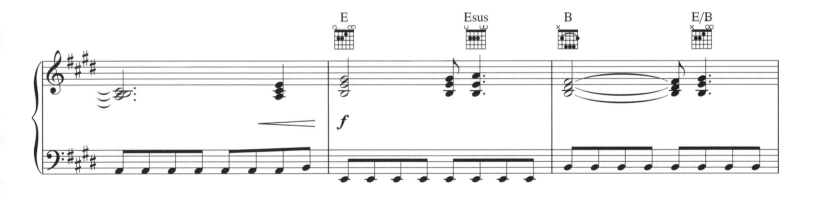

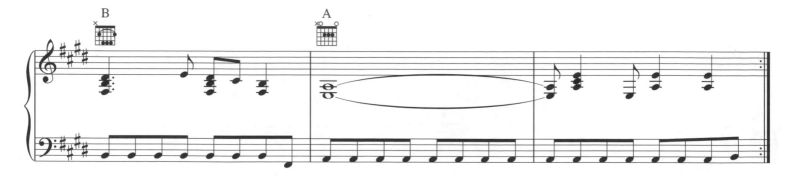

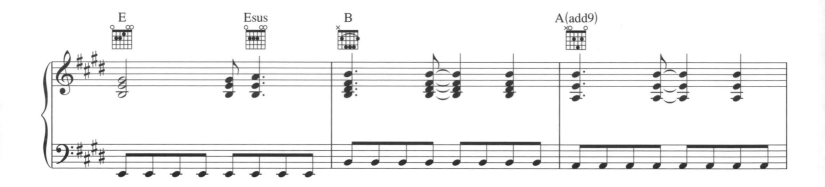

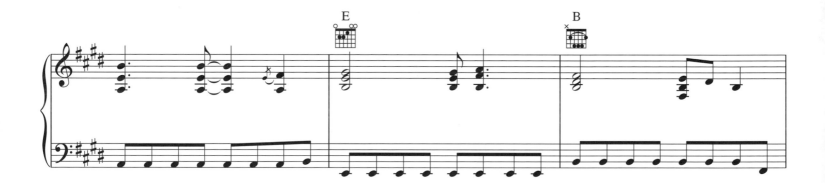

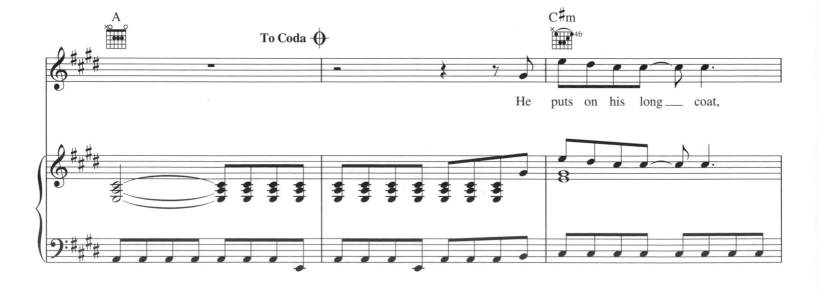

He puts on his long ___ coat,

scrib-bles off a short ___ note. Sits him-self ___ down ___ and waits ___

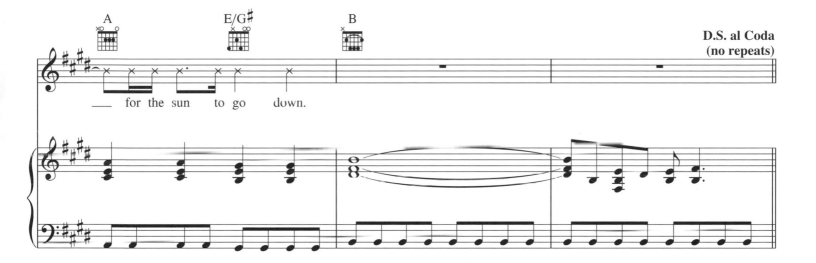

D.S. al Coda
(no repeats)

___ for the sun to go down.

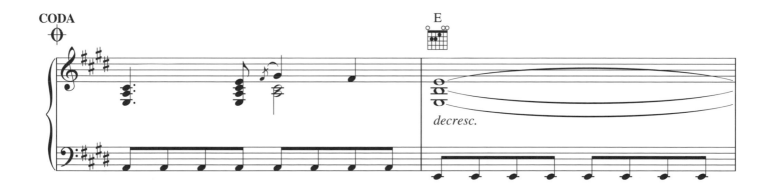

CODA

decresc.

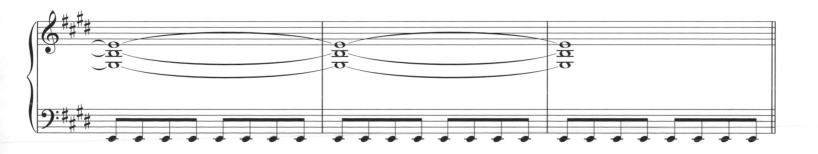

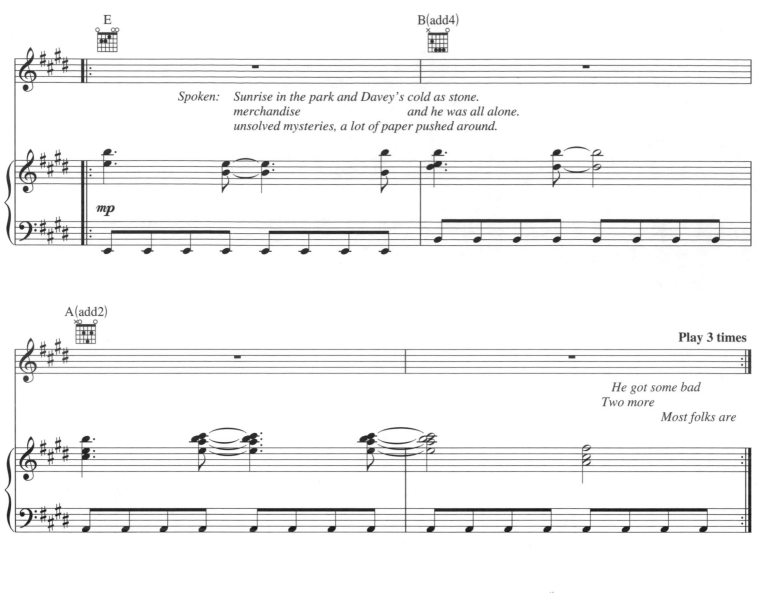

Spoken: Sunrise in the park and Davey's cold as stone.
merchandise   and he was all alone.
unsolved mysteries, a lot of paper pushed around.

mp

Play 3 times

He got some bad
Two more
            Most folks are

just waking up   *in this great big town.*

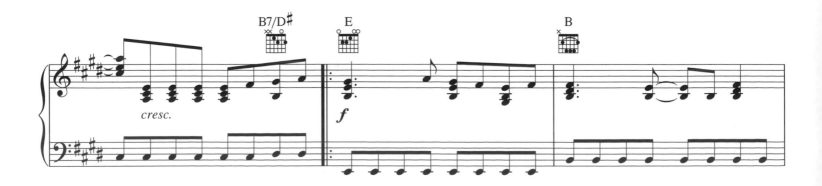

cresc.

f

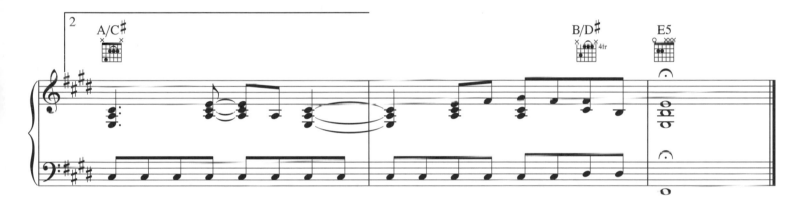

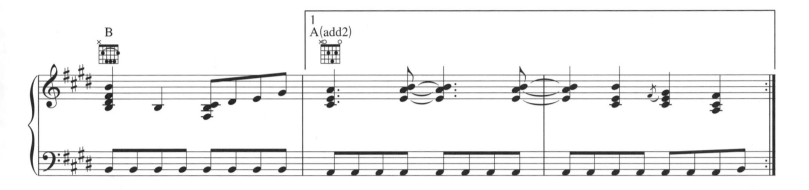

Additional Lyrics

Spoken:
3. *It's right around midnight and there's still too damn many people on this street.*
   He's walked all the way from Battery Park. He's got sweaty hands and burning feet.
   He's desperate for a fix. His body's screaming, "Get me high."
   He bursts through the door and lets one fly.

NEW COAT OF PAINT

Words and Music by
TOM WAITS

Moderately slow, with a Jazz feel

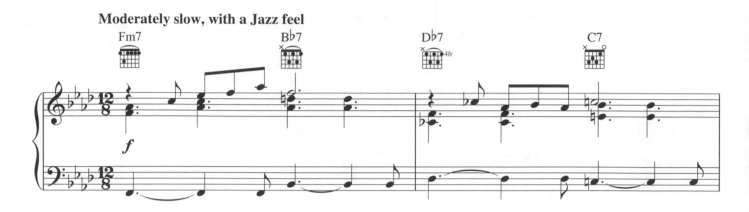

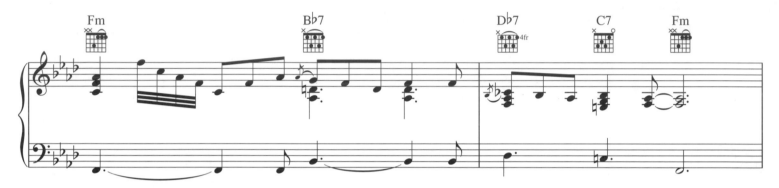

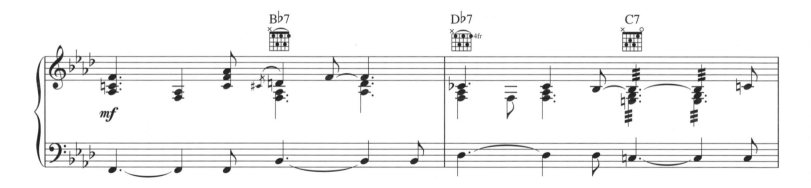

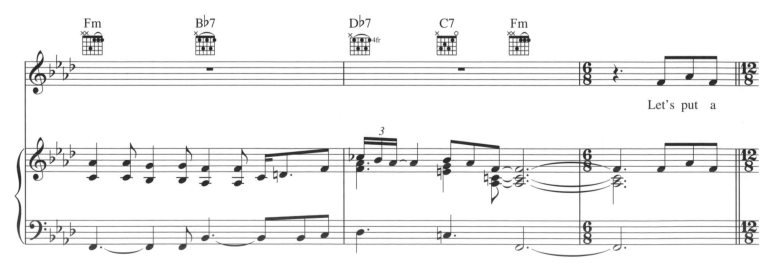

Let's put a

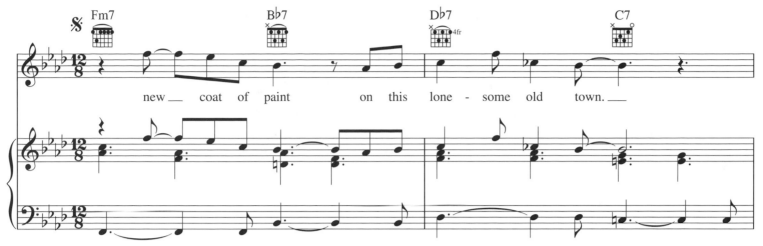

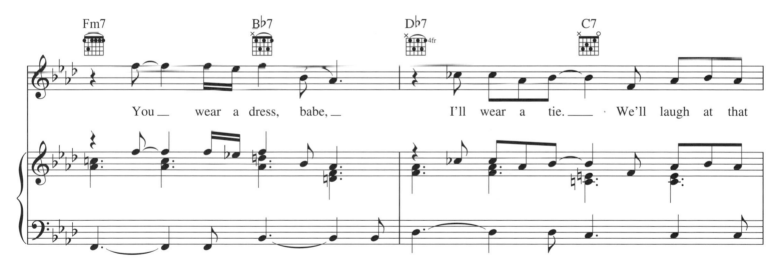

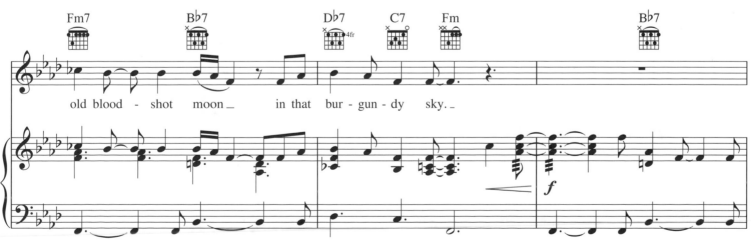

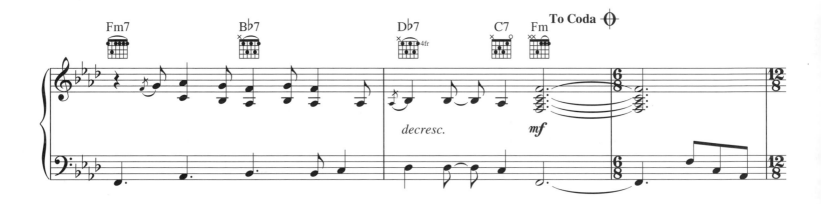

All __ our scrib - bled love dreams __ lost or thrown a - way. __

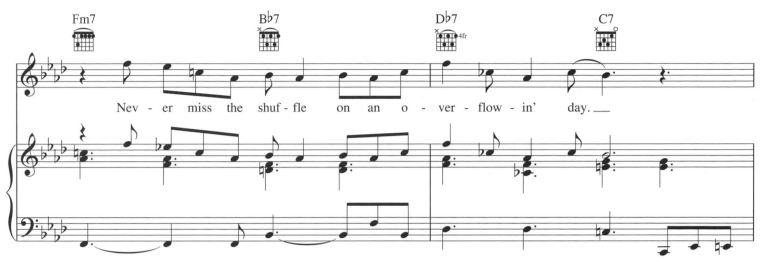

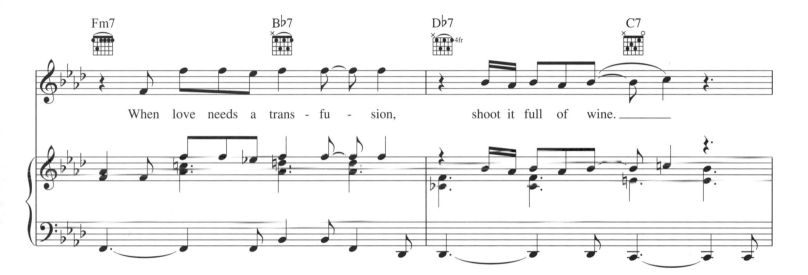

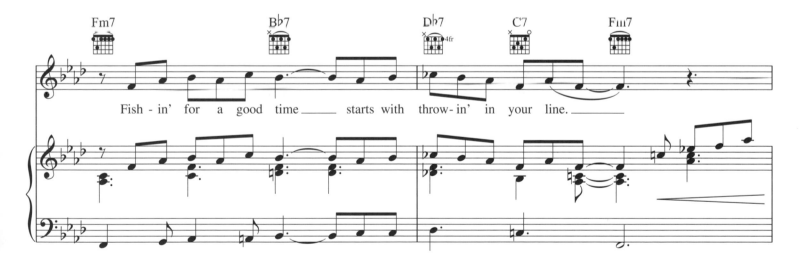

78

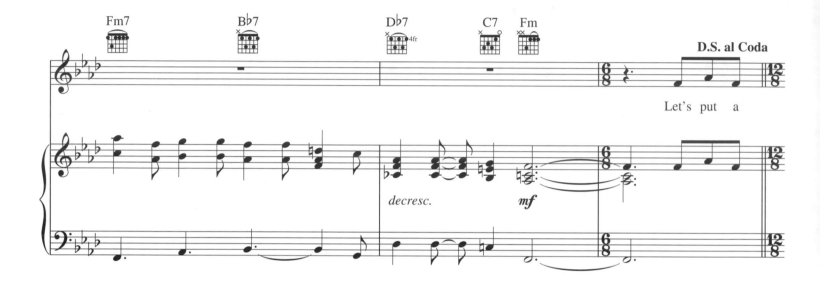

Let's put a

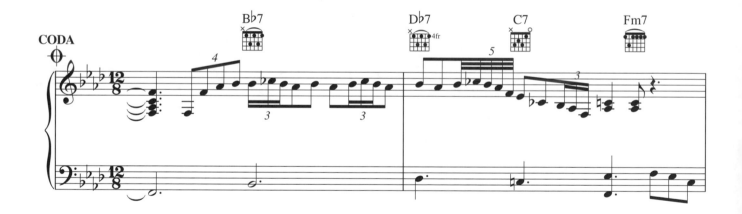

CHANCES ARE

Words and Music by
BOB SEGER

Slow Ballad

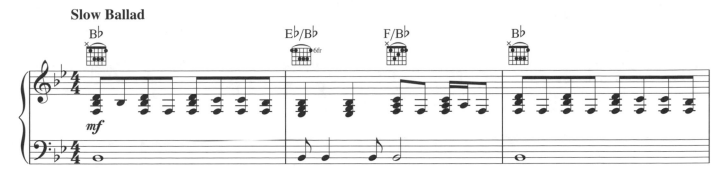

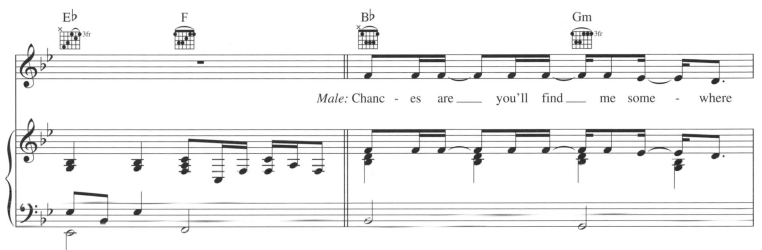

Male: Chanc - es are ___ you'll find ___ me some - where

on your road to - night. Seems I al - ways end ___ up driv - ing by. ___

Ev - er since ___ I've known ___ you it ___ just seems ___

you're on __ my way. All the rules __ of log - ic don't __ ap - ply.

I long to see __ you in __ the night,

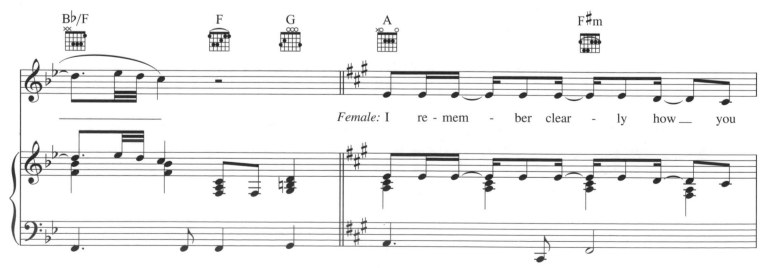

be with you __ till morn - ing light. __

Female: I re - mem - ber clear - ly how __ you

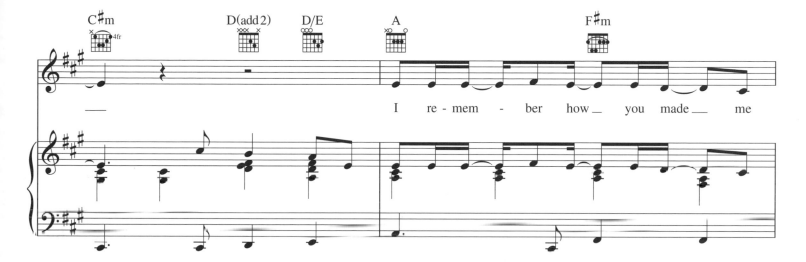

You've come to mean ___ so much ___ to me. ___

Both: Chanc - ces are ___ I'll see ___ you some - where in my dreams to - night.

You'll be smil - ing like ___ the night ___ we met.

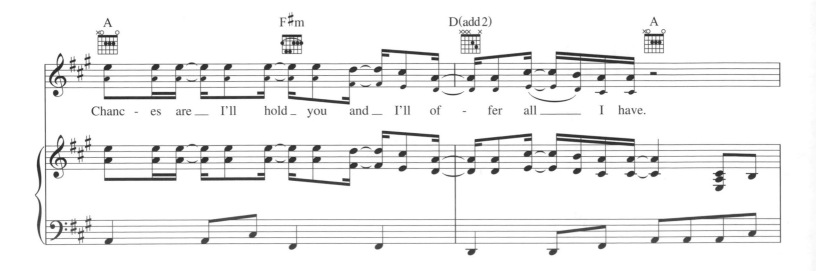

Chanc - es are ___ I'll hold ___ you and ___ I'll of - fer all _____ I have.

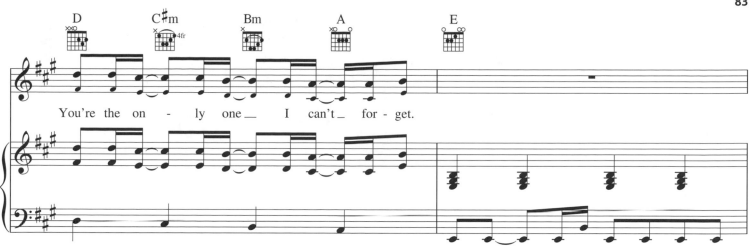

You're the on - ly one __ I can't __ for - get.

Male: Ba - by, you're __ the best I've __ ev - er met.

Both: And I'll be dream - ing of __ the fu - ture

and hop - ing you'll be by __ my side, __

Male: and in the morn-ing I'll __ be long - ing   Both: for the night, for the

night. _____   And   chanc - es are __ I'll see __ you some - where

in my dreams to - night.   You'll be smil - ing like __ the night __ we met.

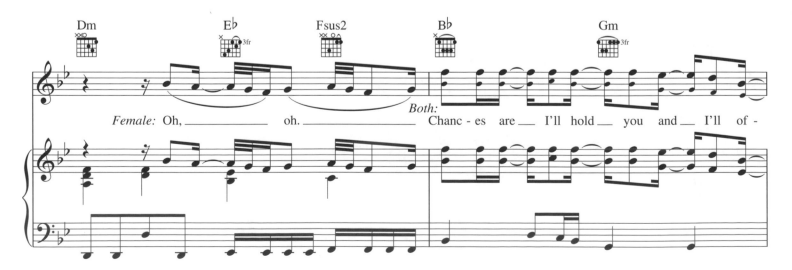

Female: Oh, _____ oh. _____   Both: Chanc - es are __ I'll hold __ you and __ I'll of -

ROCK AND ROLL NEVER FORGETS

Words and Music by
BOB SEGER

mak - in' it scream. All ___ you got to do is just make that scene ___ to - night, ___

— hey, ___ to - night. ___

Guitar solo ad lib.

D.S. al Coda

Solo ends Well now,

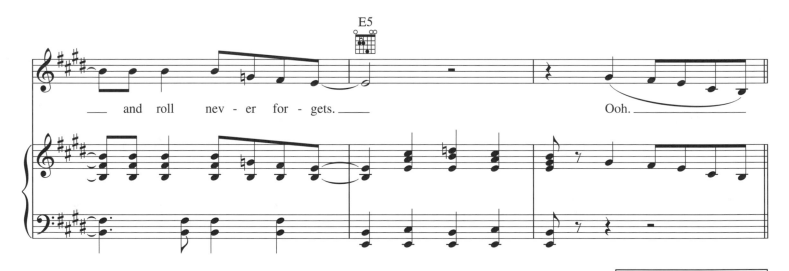

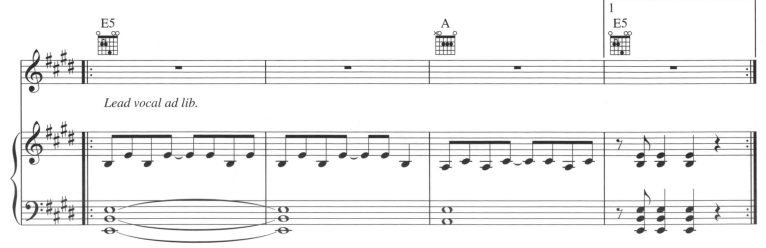

SATISFIED

Words and Music by
BOB SEGER

I need some wis - dom. ___ I need some truth.
Went to the o - cean, ___ stood in the surf.
You are the rea - son ___ that I was born.

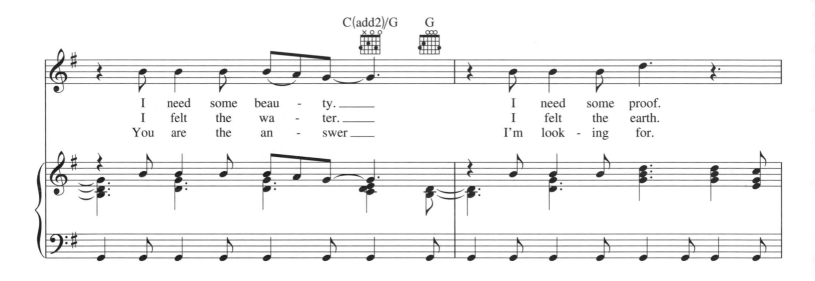

I need some beau - ty. ___ I need some proof.
I felt the wa - ter. ___ I felt the earth.
You are the an - swer ___ I'm look - ing for.

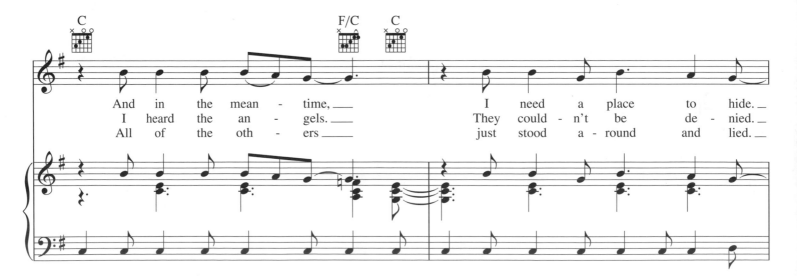

And in the mean - time, ___ I need a place to hide. ___
I heard the an - gels. ___ They could - n't be de - nied. ___
All of the oth - ers ___ just stood a - round and lied. ___

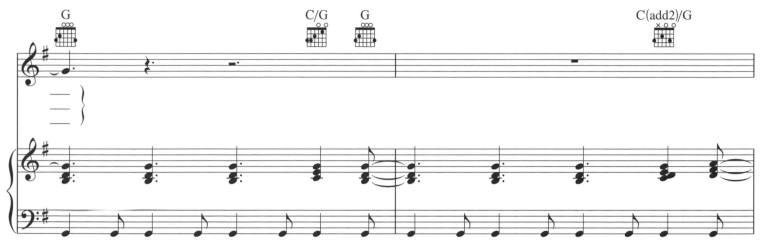

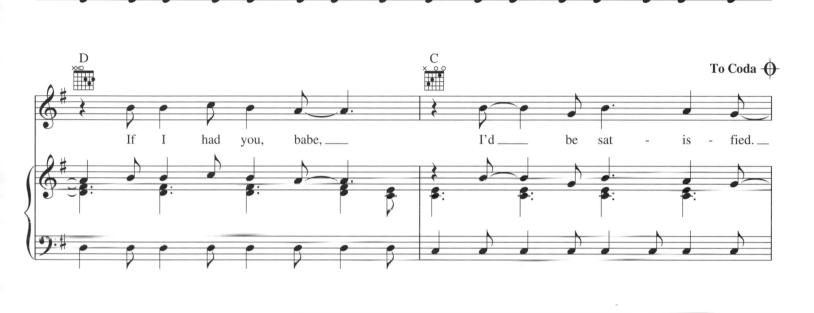

If I had you, babe, ___ I'd ___ be sat - is - fied. ___

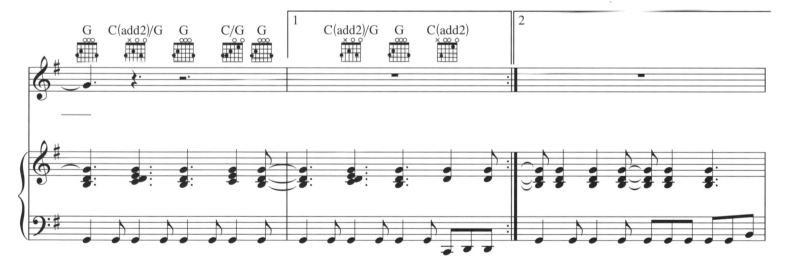

Who's gon - na be - lieve ___ me? ___ I'm a bro - ken - down ___ dog, ___

but I can still snarl with the best. ____

The train is leav - ing. ____ We can catch it if we run. ____ We can

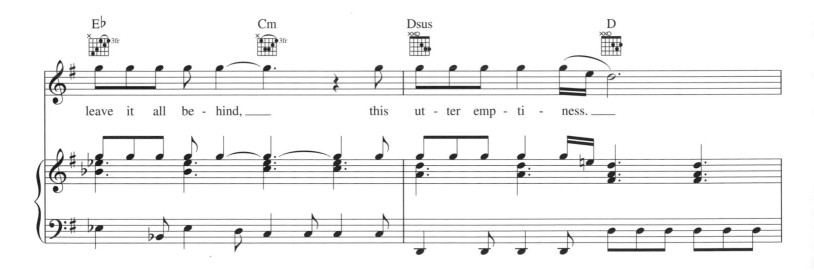

leave it all be - hind, ____ this ut - ter emp - ti - ness. ____

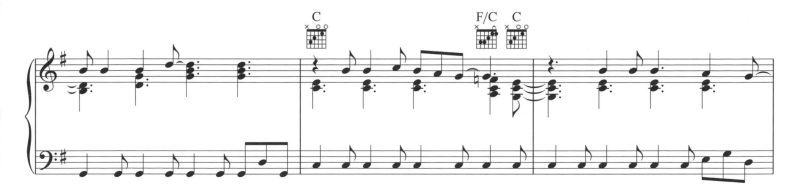

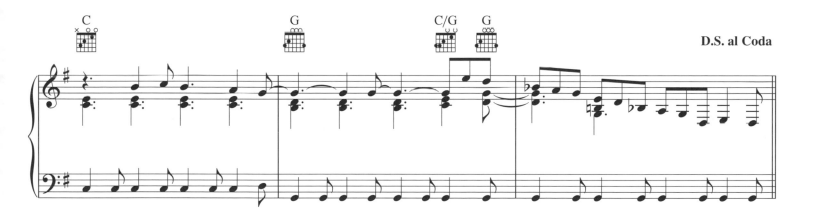

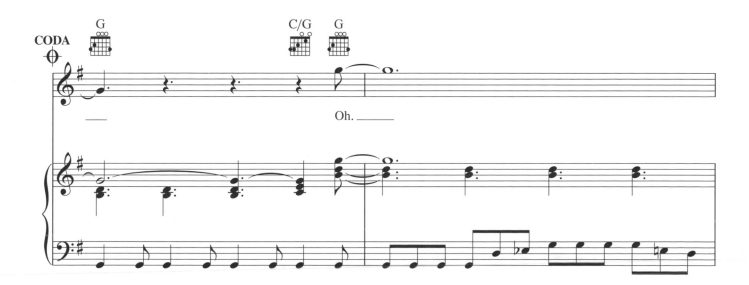

Oh. _____

96

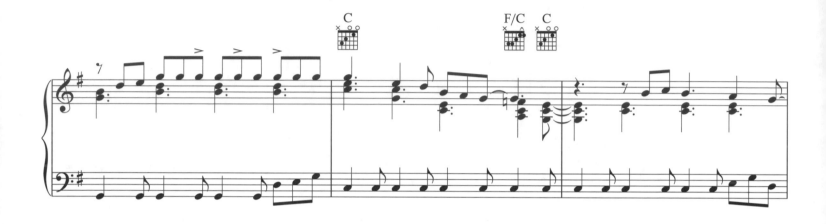

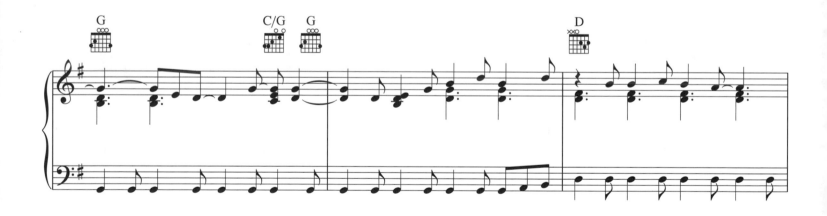

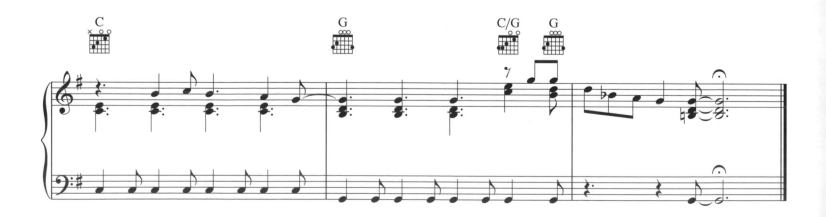

TOMORROW

Words and Music by
BOB SEGER

Moderate Rock, with a heavy feel

traf - fic in the street.　　　No more road rage.　　　No more pre -

tend - ing　　　things are real tough.

C5　　　　　　　　　G5　　　　　　　　　D5

I can't prom - ise you ___ to - mor - row. ___
I can't tell ___ you 'bout ___ to - mor - row. ___

C5　　　　　　　　　G5

No one has ___ the right ___ to lie. ___
I'm as lost ___ as yes - ter - day. ___

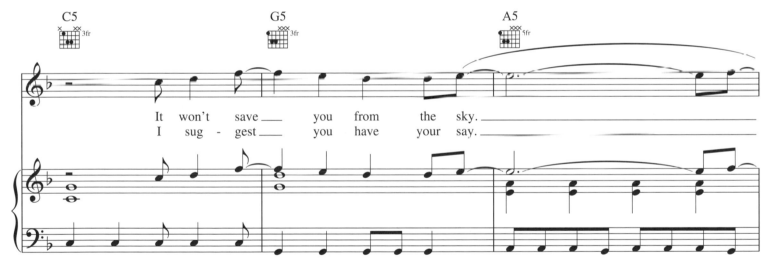

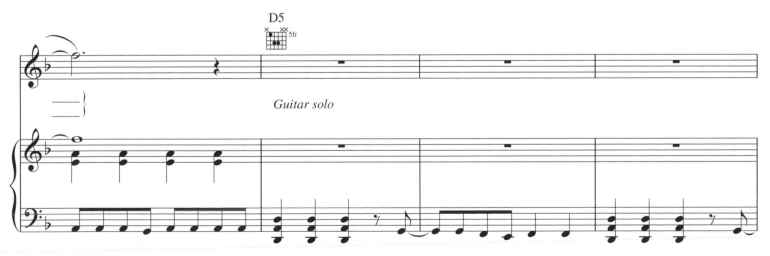

Solo ends Let me see a show of hands. __

Tell me the truth now.   What

hap - pens if __   neu - tri - nos have mass? __